OSWALD CHAMBERS

A LIFE IN PICTURES

OSWALD CHAMBERS
A LIFE IN PICTURES

PAUL KENT

Discovery House®
from Our Daily Bread Ministries

Special thanks to David McCasland for his kind assistance in reviewing this manuscript, and for his service to all of us in researching and writing *Oswald Chambers: Abandoned to God*.

Oswald Chambers: A Life in Pictures
© 2017 by Discovery House
All rights reserved.

Discovery House is affiliated with Our Daily Bread Ministries, Grand Rapids, Michigan.

Requests for permission to quote from this book should be directed to: Permissions Department, Discovery House, P.O. Box 3566, Grand Rapids, MI 49501, or contact us by email at permissionsdept@dhp.org.

Unless otherwise indicated, all Scripture quotations are taken from the King James Version.

Interior design by Sherri L. Hoffman

Library of Congress Cataloging-in-Publication Data

Names: Kent, Paul (Book editor), author.
Title: Oswald Chambers : a life in pictures / Paul Kent.
Description: Grand Rapids : Discovery House, 2017.
Identifiers: LCCN 2017036648 | ISBN 9781627077330 (hardback)
Subjects: LCSH: Chambers, Oswald, 1874-1917—Pictorial works. | Clergy—
    Great Britain—Biography—Pictorial works. | Evangelists—Great Britain—
    Biography—Pictorial works. | BISAC: BIOGRAPHY & AUTOBIOGRAPHY / Religious.
Classification: LCC BR1725.C43 K46 2017 | DDC 269/.2092 [B]—dc23
LC record available at https://lccn.loc.gov/2017036648

Printed in the United States of America

First printing in 2017

CONTENTS

Introduction / 7

1 God's Institution / 11

2 Busy, Rushing London / 19

3 The University / 29

4 Dunoon / 39

5 "Round the World All Right" / 59

6 The League of Prayer / 75

7 Beloved Disciple / 85

8 Bible Training College / 97

9 The Y.M.C.A. in Egypt / 117

10 His Ongoing Ministry / 147

Appendix A: Timeline of Oswald Chambers's Life and Work / 157

Appendix B: Bibliography—The Complete Works of Oswald Chambers / 161

Sources / 165

Photography Credits / 166

*Shut out every other consideration and keep
yourself before God for this one thing only—
"My Utmost for His Highest." I am determined to be
absolutely and entirely for Him and for Him alone.*

INTRODUCTION

From opposite points on the globe they were called to a military camp in the Egyptian desert—soldiers from Australia and New Zealand, following orders of the British Empire, and a preacher from Scotland, obeying a far higher Authority.

Oswald Chambers arrived in Egypt in late October 1915, with much of Europe and the Middle East in the throes of World War I. "I am more relieved than horrified that war has come," he had written a friend the year before. "The immediate result among many men is that much irresponsible pleasure-seeking and frivolity is ended . . . and men everywhere are more open to talk about God, the soul, and final issues than heretofore." Wartime Egypt was a good setting for "dealing with God," as Chambers said of two soldiers who, shortly after his arrival, "came beautifully through to Jesus Christ."

From his home base—a Y.M.C.A. camp at Zeitoun, a few miles northeast of Cairo—Chambers exemplified Jesus to the Colonial soldiers, and the occasional Tommies, as servicemen of the home island were called. For just over two years, until his death on November 15, 1917, he befriended, encouraged, and interceded for the "big, fine, hearty fellows" he described in his diary. And he taught them the Bible with insight, clarity, and clock-like regularity.

Chambers in Egypt, wearing the broad-brimmed hat of his Australian soldiers.

Gertrude "Biddy" Chambers, approximately ten years after Oswald's death, and the typewriter on which she produced the manuscripts for his books.

A full century after, much of Oswald Chambers's stature in the Christian world derives from these "talks" he had with the men—or similar lessons shared at his Bible Training College or in a Pentecostal League of Prayer meeting. Each was carefully recorded in shorthand by his wife, Biddy, who would later collate and edit his words, producing many of the books and booklets that bear his name—some four dozen in all.

In one of his final lessons, spoken shortly before the appendicitis attack that led to his death, Chambers said "the influence of one man of integrity over men is incalculable." His example was the "Beloved Captain" of British soldier and author Donald Hankey, but the quote truly encapsulates Chambers's own life: men (and women) of integrity had influenced him, and he went on to exert an immeasurable spiritual influence on the people around him.

Though he lived only forty-three years, Chambers's influence continues today—most notably through the daily devotional *My Utmost for His Highest*. The "Golden Book of Oswald Chambers" has been read and pondered by pastors and Christian musicians, business leaders and members of the media, a U.S. Senate chaplain, and a sitting president . . . in addition to everyday believers around the world, in numbers known only to God.

So who exactly was this man? What kind of home life and education contributed to his moral and intellectual development? How did his teaching ministry begin and grow? Why is he more widely known a hundred years after his death than he ever was in life?

8 Oswald Chambers: A Life in Pictures

Oswald Chambers: A Life in Pictures offers insight into the influence of his family and friends, the places he lived and schools he attended, the organizations he served and experiences he had, all of which helped to fashion a remarkable life and ministry. But the book also chronicles the other side of influence, that of Chambers's effect on individuals, churches, and organizations, which began early in his life and has only grown after his death. Chambers's experience, and our experience of him, are presented here in both text and photographs. Each chapter begins with a narrative account, which is followed by "Scenes from His Life," a section of supporting photographs.

It is our hope that by knowing Oswald Chambers more deeply, you might also draw closer to his Lord, Jesus Christ. As Chambers himself said, "The one test of a teacher sent from God is that those who listen see and know Jesus Christ better than they ever did. If you are a teacher sent from God your worth in God's sight is estimated by the way you enable people to see Jesus."

May you see Jesus in this account of His servant Oswald Chambers.

Paul Kent
Discovery House

Oswald, Biddy, and their only child, Kathleen, at the Bible Training College, London, in 1915. Oswald would leave for Egypt that October; by the end of the year, the family would be together again at Zeitoun.

Introduction   9

Rooftops of Aberdeen, Scotland, Oswald Chambers's birthplace. The spire of the Kirk of Saint Nicholas is seen at right. A previous church building was destroyed by fire in 1874, the year Chambers was born.

1 GOD'S INSTITUTION

*Home is God's institution, and He says,
"Honour thy father and thy mother";
are we fulfilling our duty to our parents
as laid down in God's Book?*

OSWALD CHAMBERS, *Biblical Ethics*

Historical figures tend to occupy our memory as fully formed men and women, recalled from the days of their greatest achievements. Those familiar with Oswald Chambers likely envision him as a thirty- or forty-year-old man, as the preacher, the teacher, the army chaplain, the mind behind *My Utmost for His Highest*. It's harder to imagine him as the "chubby infant" his brother Ernest described, or as a little boy eagerly asking God for guinea pigs.

But the intellectual and spiritual giant who would ultimately earn worldwide fame began life just like everyone else—as a baby. Oswald was the eighth of nine children born to Clarence and Hannah Chambers; an older sister had died in infancy, so six siblings welcomed his arrival on July 24, 1874.

From the moment he entered the world, Oswald Chambers enjoyed the benefits of a Christian home. His parents, three brothers, and, eventually, four sisters constituted "God's institution," as Oswald would one day describe the family, his first great influence in life.

He and his siblings were PKs—preacher's kids—and Clarence was pastoring in Aberdeen, Scotland, when Oswald was born. The elder Chambers was the tenth and, to that point, the longest serving minister (1866–77) of the Crown Terrace Baptist Church.

Photographs of Pastor Chambers show a stern-looking man, an interpretation supported by Franklin's comment that "Father was very strict in our upbringing." Oswald's daughter, Kathleen, would recall her grandfather as "completely and utterly humorless . . . a dour, dour Scot who preached hellfire."

Clarence Chambers was balanced by his wife, Hannah, who was "loving and gentle and very, very sweet," in Kathleen's recollection. Years after Oswald's death in Egypt, Franklin recalled a family life filled with games: "We found our enjoyment and entertainment in our own home; no outside amusements could possibly compare with the fun and happiness to be found there."

The Chambers home could trace its spiritual lineage through the famed British pastor Charles Haddon Spurgeon. "The Prince of Preachers," whose Metropolitan Tabernacle in London held six thousand people, had baptized both Clarence and Hannah and had ordained Clarence to the ministry after he'd attended Spurgeon's Pastors' College. Ultimately, Clarence's oldest and youngest sons—Arthur and Oswald—would follow him into full-time Christian service.

· · ·

An early portrait of Oswald and his sister Gertrude (right), and (above) the entire Chambers family in the mid-1880s: Clarence and Hannah surrounded by (clockwise from lower left) Florence, Gertrude, Bertha, Arthur, Ernest, Edith, Franklin, and Oswald.

12 Oswald Chambers: A Life in Pictures

When Oswald was born, his siblings ranged in age from thirteen to two. "None divined him different than the rest," the third oldest, Ernest, wrote in a poem shortly after Oswald's death:

He was our brother, and we never guessed
Nor marked him for the "chosen vessel" blest
He later would become.

But Oswald's spiritual nature soon drew his family's notice. "As a child his prayers were very original," Franklin recalled, "and frequently when he had gone to bed . . . the older members of the family, including his mother, would listen on the stairs to hear him pray." Oswald's petition for pets, offered "night after night," was ultimately answered with two guinea pigs in the chicken coop. Franklin didn't record who put them there but wrote that Oswald's "delight was great." This childlike confidence in God would continue throughout his entire life and ministry.

In time, like the brothers of Jesus, the Chambers siblings came to understand Oswald's uniqueness. "He was our brother once, now he was more—God spake to us through him," Ernest wrote:

He was our brother still, but he was, too,
God's minister to us, his words rang true,
He taught the way of Life like one who knew,
For he had walked with Him.

. . .

Oswald Chambers (sitting, center) at age twelve, with his three older brothers. Arthur (standing), twenty-five at the time of the photo, became a Baptist minister in Eltham, just east of London; Oswald's future wife, Gertrude Hobbs, was part of Arthur's congregation. Ernest (left), nineteen in this photo, became an artist in a china factory. Franklin (right), sixteen, became a chemist in a dye plant. Much of our knowledge of Oswald's early years comes from the account Franklin wrote for the 1933 book compiled by Biddy, *Oswald Chambers: His Life and Work.*

God's Institution

When Oswald was five years old, the Chambers family moved from Aberdeen, on the North Sea, to the interior of England, nearly three hundred miles south. At Stoke-on-Trent, the heart of the nation's pottery industry, Clarence Chambers served two years as Home Missions Evangelist for the North Staffordshire Baptist Association, helping start a small church in nearby Fenton, before accepting a call back to Scotland. For the next eight years, until Oswald was fifteen, Clarence led the Baptist Chapel of Perth, a small city some seventy miles southwest of Aberdeen.

For a growing boy, Perth offered many pleasures. "During that time Oswald laid in a fine stock of health, running about the hillsides and along by the River Tay to the beautiful Woody Island," Franklin wrote. Perth was also the place of Oswald's first schooling outside the home, at Sharp's Institution.

Franklin said Oswald began showing a gift for drawing at this point in his life, "and this became his main joy at school." Interestingly, "the intense brain power of later life was not evident in those early days and he never won a prize while at school." Even more interesting, to the age of fifteen Oswald Chambers had not made a profession of faith in Christ.

Born, like Oswald Chambers, in 1874

- Winston Churchill (British prime minister, 1940–45, '51–55)
- Herbert Hoover (U.S. president, 1929–33)
- G. K. Chesterton (British critic and author, creator of the Father Brown mysteries)
- Erich Weiss (Hungarian-American magician better known as Harry Houdini)
- Lucy Maud Montgomery (Canadian author of *Anne of Green Gables*)
- Guglielmo Marconi (Italian physicist, known for the development of radio)
- Howard Carter (British archaeologist, discoverer of King Tutankhamen's tomb)
- Robert Frost (U.S. poet)

OPPOSITE: The city center of Perth, Scotland, is reflected on the River Tay. Oswald Chambers lived in Perth between the ages of seven and fifteen, while his father served as a Baptist pastor.

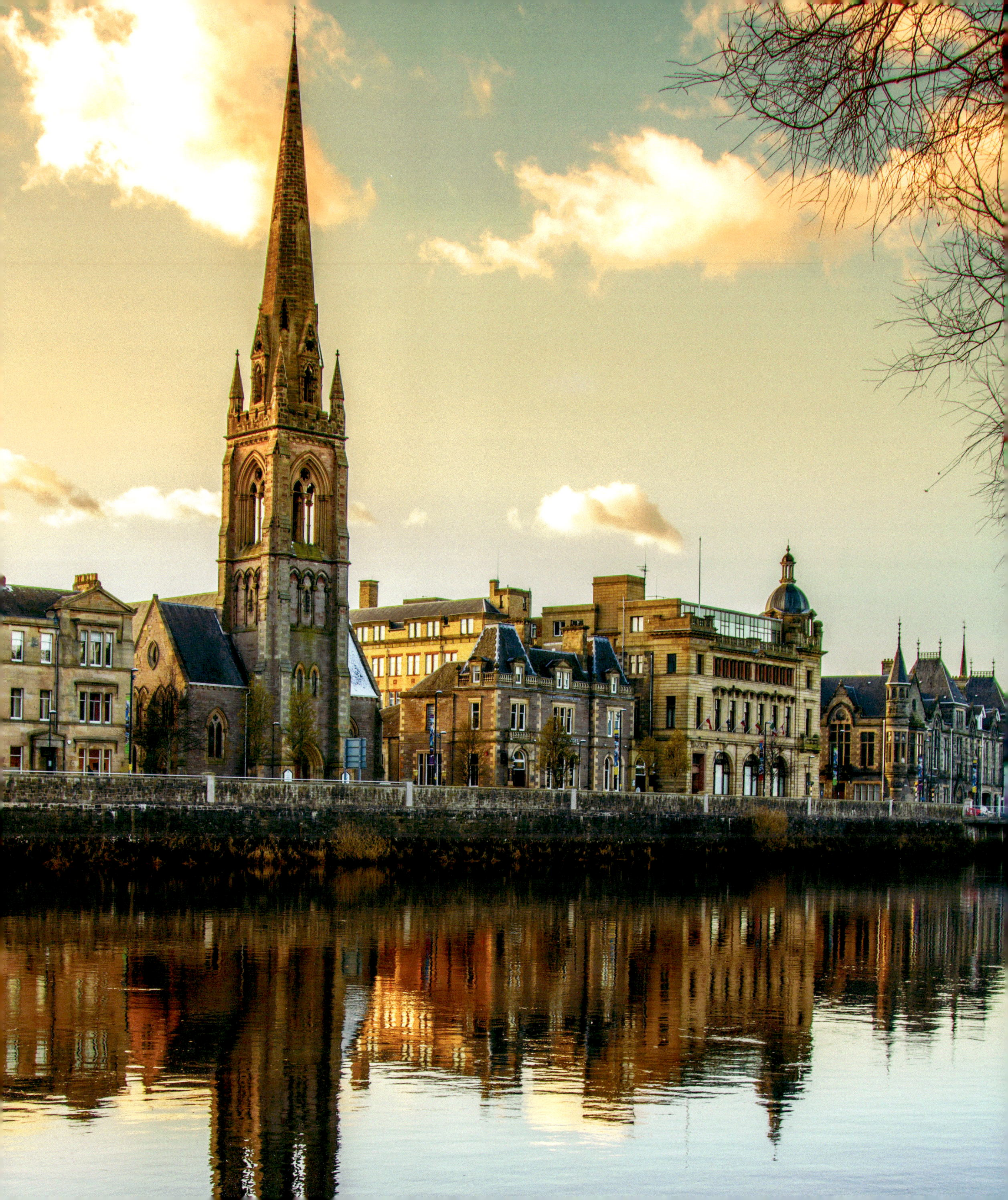

SCENES FROM HIS LIFE

An undated photo of Clarence Chambers. Oswald's father trained for the ministry at Charles Spurgeon's Pastors' College in London, taking his first church in Romsey, about seventy miles southwest of London. Then he spent twelve years in Aberdeen, Scotland's Crown Terrace Baptist Church, resigning after the congregation complained of "dissatisfaction and non-profiting" from his ministry. Oswald was not quite three at the time.

When Oswald began his own ministry, he and Clarence would have differences over money. While teaching at Dunoon, Scotland, Oswald wrote his father saying, "I know you would not hold the attitude you do regarding my present circumstances if you saw things as I do. 'Worthy of my hire!' Why, I have more than I deserve even of money. I have leisure to work at my will, and the opportunity of helping men towards realizing their call to the ministry, and I have the inward conviction that I am doing God's will. I could, as you say, earn money elsewhere, but what is money-help compared to the eternal assistance I may be enabled to give to souls?"

"My father loved my grandfather very much," Kathleen Chambers recalled decades later, "but of course, they disagreed, you see, very, very fundamentally and very strongly."

In lessons he taught at the Bible Training College and the Zeitoun camp in Egypt (which became the book *The Psychology of Redemption*), Oswald said, "If the mother of our Lord misunderstood Him, and His brethren did not believe in Him, the same things will happen to His life in us, and we must not think it strange concerning the misunderstandings of others. The life of the Son of God in us is brought into the same kind of circumstances that the historic life of Jesus Christ was brought into, and what was true of Him will be true also of His life in us."

16   Oswald Chambers: A Life in Pictures

Clarence and Hannah Chambers on their fiftieth wedding anniversary, July 16, 1910. Franklin reported that Oswald "was always a great boy for his home and his Mother, she had a big influence on his life and his devotion to her increased as he grew older." On her birthday in 1917, only weeks before his death, Oswald wrote, "All that formed my ideas of woman (and I have great ideas) is from you; all that entered (all unconsciously) into my conceptions of Motherhood and home-training, and comfort and sagacious sunshine, has been formed in me by you."

In a September 26, 1906, letter to Hannah (whom he addressed as "My dear 'brick' of a Mother"), Oswald expressed appreciation for his parents' support—even if they were sometimes bewildered by his choices:

> *If it is possible, I love you more than ever for being so robust and strong in your mind. Thank God for you and upon every remembrance of you. God surely has wonderfully answered your prayers for your children. The memory of Mother's doings and managings are to me a growing stimulus and an amazement, while her detestation of cant and humbug also seems to have left in me no little of the same spirit. I, as your youngest son, see you both transfigured in the light of years and life. I thank God for you, and praise Him that neither of you ever offered any obstacle to my following out what appeared to me God's calls, for the ways and turnings have perplexed you much, but, thank God, He has allowed you to live to see that when He leads all is well.*

When he left home for his university studies, Oswald wrote, "I feel traits in my character I knew not of before and it causes me to bow in deeper gratitude for that home training which I have now left for the training and discipline of life. Oh, what a mighty influence home life has on us! Indeed, we do not know how deep a debt we owe to our mothers and fathers and their training."

God's Institution 17

Rye Lane, the main business street of Peckham, a district of southeast London where Oswald Chambers moved with his parents and two sisters in 1889. Oswald would be baptized by the Reverend J. T. Briscoe in the Rye Lane Baptist Chapel.

2 BUSY, RUSHING LONDON

Busy, driving, rushing Londoners,
Driven, palefaced, wiry blunderers,
Striving ever,
Praying never,
Busy, driving, rushing Londoners.

OSWALD CHAMBERS, *"Londoners"*

Life changed dramatically for Oswald Chambers in 1889. With his parents and the two sisters closest to him in age—Gertrude and Florence—the fifteen-year-old moved from the small Scottish city of Perth to the largest metropolis on the planet: London.

The family stepped into a city roiled a year earlier by the infamous serial killer "Jack the Ripper." It was the London of Sir Arthur Conan Doyle's fictional detective Sherlock Holmes, a bustling, sprawling place of some six million residents, running the gamut from opulent wealth to intense squalor. As the Holmes character Dr. John Watson described a journey across it, the city comprised "fashionable London, hotel London, theatrical London, literary London, commercial London, and finally maritime London," rimmed by riverside neighborhoods of a hundred thousand souls, "where the tenement houses swelter and reek."

From his home in the southeastern suburb of Peckham, Oswald Chambers watched his fellow Londoners with interest, describing them in a poem he wrote in April 1894. The third verse describes

Tired out, weary, haggard Londoners
Beer-sopped, feeble, worn-out conjurers,
Struggling ever,
Resting never,
Tired out, weary, haggard Londoners.

Compared with his later, more sympathetic approach to fellow travelers, Oswald's four-stanza poem seems uncharacteristically downbeat—especially its very last line, "silent, lifeless, buried Londoners." Perhaps he was beginning to view others' lives with apprehension now that he himself had been reborn in Christ.

Like that of his parents before him, Oswald Chambers's spiritual life was influenced by the Reverend Charles Spurgeon. Shortly after arriving in London, according to his brother Franklin, Oswald went with his father to a Spurgeon service, "and on the way home he said that had there been an opportunity he would have given himself to the Lord. Father said at once, 'You can do it now, my boy,' and then and there he gave himself to God."

TOP: Charles Haddon Spurgeon (1834–92), became pastor of London's New Park Street Chapel in 1854 at age twenty; by 1861, he was preaching to crowds of six thousand in the newly constructed Metropolitan Tabernacle. Oswald Chambers accepted Christ after hearing Spurgeon speak.

LEFT: Interior of the Metropolitan Tabernacle, showing Spurgeon's pulpit at center.

20 Oswald Chambers: A Life in Pictures

By the end of the next year, on December 2, 1890, Oswald would be baptized and join the Rye Lane Baptist Chapel, only a short distance from his home. The church's pastor, Reverend J. T. Briscoe, was known to encourage young believers to share their faith, which Oswald soon did. "He began to enter into Church life and became a teacher in the Sunday School," Franklin wrote years later. Oswald was introduced to lodging-house work, Franklin said, "and much time was spent visiting the men, some of them ex-convicts, and speaking to them of Christ."

Before long, Oswald was speaking in other venues, too. Chrissie Brain, a fellow member of the Rye Lane church who became Oswald's girlfriend for several years, was present for many of his "youthful addresses." His first, on Isaiah 55:1, was preached "in a crowded thoroughfare in Peckham." There were many others, including a talk to parents at a Sunday school social when Oswald was all of eighteen years old. "It was the best address to parents I ever heard," Chrissie reported, "but its precocity was somewhat staggering!"

Though his teaching was "much appreciated," according to a fellow worker at Peckham's Relf Road Mission, Oswald poured himself into all kinds of ministry work. "My recollection of him," the man said, "is of a cheery, greathearted and stalwart colleague, always ready to assist in any way within his power."

. . .

Oswald Chambers, age sixteen, in a portrait taken in a Peckham studio. In this year of his life he would be baptized, join a church, and begin teaching and preaching God's Word.

Busy, Rushing London

Oswald Chambers's portrait of the German composer Ludwig von Beethoven (1770–1827). Chambers created the image, done in charcoal, when he was eighteen or nineteen.

Still only a teenager, Oswald Chambers longed for an education that would polish and enlarge his innate creativity. His father was wary of the art world but ultimately allowed Oswald to enter the National Art Training School, six miles northwest of Peckham in South Kensington. There, he would pursue the Art Master's Certificate that would allow him to teach in a school—though Oswald was feeling a much larger call:

My life work, as I see it, my eternal work, is, in the Almighty strength of God, to strike for the redemption of the Aesthetic Kingdom—Music and Art and Poetry—or rather, the proving of Christ's redemption of it. . . . As far as my limited knowledge goes, our Master and Saviour has no representative to "teach, reprove and exhort," and an ambition, a longing, has seized me, seized me so powerfully that it has convinced me of the need. The Spirit of God seems to cry—"Whom shall I send, and who will go for us?" Then, through all my weaknesses, my sinfulness, and my frailties, my soul cried— "Here am I, send me."

By his twenty-first birthday, July 24, 1895, Oswald Chambers was ready for the next phase of his personal development—a two-year arts course at the University of Edinburgh, back in his native Scotland.

◆—◇—◆

SCENES FROM HIS LIFE

"The Prince of Preachers," Charles Spurgeon, around the time of Oswald Chambers's birth. Spurgeon had baptized both of Oswald's parents, and Clarence Chambers had studied at Spurgeon's college for pastors. When Oswald was fifteen, newly arrived in London, he heard Spurgeon speak and afterward, on the way home with his father, accepted Christ.

The quiet, unassuming conversion offered no hint of the powerful ministry to come, but years later, when he taught at the Bible Training College in Clapham (1911–15), Oswald would say, "Extraordinary conversions and phenomenal experiences are magnificent specimen studies of what happens in the life of everyone, but not one in a million has an experience such as the Apostle Paul had. The majority of us are unnoticed and unnoticeable people." Humility, he would say on another occasion, "is the one stamp of a saint."

Spurgeon would die three years after Oswald's conversion, unaware of the far-reaching impact of that particular sermon.

Metropolitan Tabernacle

Busy, Rushing London

SCENES FROM HIS LIFE

Rye Lane Chapel, Peckham, England, the first church Oswald Chambers attended that was not pastored by his father. In late 1890, at the age of sixteen, Oswald was baptized and joined this congregation, pastored by J. T. Briscoe. "What deep and grateful memories I have of that man of God," Chambers wrote when "Pa Briscoe" died in 1917, "he meant a mighty lot to me in my spiritual life in the days before I went to Edinburgh."

After Oswald died in 1917, fellow church member Robert Flaherty recalled that "he used to attend the weekly prayer meetings regularly; for some time he did not take any part, but eventually he broke through. His prayers at first were crude, just a sentence or two, but they were expressions which laid hold of one; more than once I heard him say, 'O Lord, drench us with humility.' A great prayer for one so young." Describing Oswald Chambers as "an out-and-out worker," Flaherty said, "even in those early days we were convinced that God had anointed him for special service."

24 Oswald Chambers: A Life in Pictures

Contrasting with the clean, polished appearance of the Rye Lane chapel were the "missions" where young Oswald Chambers often worked. Pastor J. T. Briscoe urged his congregation to participate in evangelism in working-class areas—this "proposed new mission hall" was on Sumner Road, north of the church. As Robert Flaherty recalled, "It was my pleasure to go with [Oswald Chambers] to the common lodging-houses located in South London. He was always an ardent worker among the down-and-out; these men appealed to him, and perhaps gave him a deeper insight into the power of sin to degrade, and also the greater power of the grace of God to break the power of cancelled sin and redeem men to Himself."

John Thatcher, who met Chambers a decade after his Rye Lane days and described himself as "down and out" when he came to Christ, called Oswald "my spiritual father, my succourer, my friend and counsellor." Just shy of forty, "having led a drunken and godless life," Thatcher was suddenly and obviously converted. "From the first Oswald Chambers sought me out and took me in hand. How I thank God for his help, and for the hours he spent on his knees wrestling with God on my behalf. He taught me to pray; he opened up the Scriptures to me, and patiently laboured in the exposition of the Bible truth until I was rooted and grounded in the Word of God. Oswald Chambers held the secrets of God, and truly he prevailed with man for God and with God for man."

Busy, Rushing London

SCENES FROM HIS LIFE

Oswald Chambers's sojourn in London included a course of study at the National Art Training School, later called the Royal College of Art, in South Kensington. He performed well enough to earn a scholarship for a two-year study abroad, "but having seen men come back from their travels moral and physical wrecks, he refused the scholarship," his brother Franklin recalled.

In time, and with considerable struggle, he would give up his artistic dreams to become a full-time minister.

Undated sketches by Oswald Chambers. In a lecture he gave at the Bible Training College (1911–15), Chambers defined an *artist* as "one who not only sees but is prepared to pay the price of acquiring the technical knowledge to express what he sees." An *artistic person*, on the other hand, "is one who has not enough art in him to make him work at the technique of art whereby he can express himself; he indulges in moods and tones and impressions; consequently there are more artistic people than there are artists. . . . Unless he goes into the concentrated, slogging business of learning the technique of expression, his genius will be of no use to anyone."

26   Oswald Chambers: A Life in Pictures

When he was twenty-one, Oswald Chambers made this pencil sketch of his London friend George Oxer. As with many of Chambers's associates, Oxer wrote a reminiscence for the 1933 book *Oswald Chambers: His Life and Work*, recalling, "I was Oswald Chambers' chum, as far as his somewhat unique soul could have a chum, for some years when both of us were in the late teens and early twenties. The fact that he espied angels where I saw only a fence did not militate against a real friendship. Each to the other was a fellow-flounderer in wayside bogs not unfamiliar to travelers along the road of the great 'Quest.' I used to run my doubts full tilt at him, and can even now feel his arm grip mine and hear the urge of his spirit in the Scotch of his voice, 'Courage, lad.'"

Oswald Chambers loved the poetry of Robert Browning (1812–89), who he called a "grand, manly thinker." George Oxer recalled that Chambers "was dining most happily and somewhat voraciously at the table of the poet Browning, and his 'titbits' of Robert were constantly passed on to me for my delectation, but I fear that my felicity was sometimes more assumed than actual. Yet how easy it was in those early days to detect the brave soul beating behind the brain in turmoil, battling with the 'tugs.'"

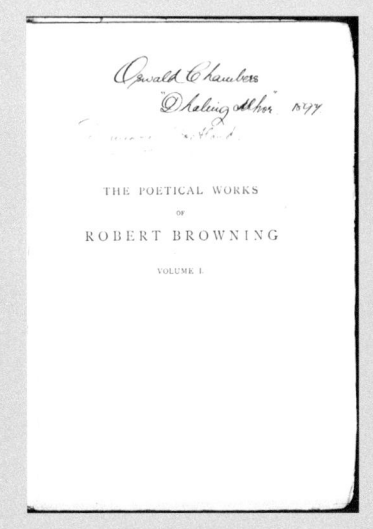

"The tugs" is a reference to Browning's long poem "Easter-Day," which says, in part,

> *How very hard it is to be*
> *A Christian! Hard for you and me,*
> *. . .*
> *And the sole thing that I remark*
> *Upon the difficulty, this,*
> *We do not see it where it is,*
> *At the beginning of the race:*
> *As we proceed, it shifts its place,*
> *And where we looked for palms to fall,*
> *We find the tug's to come,—that's all.*

These seeds of struggle in his late teens would one day develop into a years-long crisis that Chambers described as "hell on earth."

Busy, Rushing London 27

Oswald Chambers, as a student at the University of Edinburgh in the 1895–96 school year. He would lodge in a room previously used by the well-known preacher John Henry Jowett, and Franklin said, "We prayed that some of his spirit might pass to Oswald."

3 THE UNIVERSITY

I made very satisfactory progress last week, work is prosperous, my studies at the University most delightful, and my health of body and vigour of mind were never what they are now.

OSWALD CHAMBERS, *letter of Fall 1895*

After six years in London, Oswald Chambers was thrilled with the opportunity to return to the land of his birth.

"Scotland, all hail!" he rhapsodized. "How my soul beats and strains and yearns for you; Scotland, bonnie, bonnie Scotland, how I love you!" A two-year program at the University of Edinburgh awaited him, but he would gain much more than an education—there he would also hear an unmistakable call of God to the ministry.

His experience in Edinburgh began happily, as indicated by the excerpt above, from a letter to his girlfriend, Chrissie Brain. Oswald appreciated his landlords, a Christian couple named Bell he would later identify as honorary grandparents. "These people," he wrote, "will have a great influence on my life, I'm certain."

He made his rented room a chamber of solitary study: "I do not know any of the students," Oswald wrote to Chrissie. "I live by myself, in myself, and to myself." But this disengagement was only a temporary thing, he said, "that ultimately I may be all for others and my Master."

Coursework in moral philosophy, ethics, psychology, and British literature, all taught by leading professors in the various fields, challenged Chambers's eager mind and spirit. After a year of study in Edinburgh, he would say, "it will ever be one of the most important and influential years of my life."

But God would also use other "teachers" to develop Oswald Chambers. By his first spring in Edinburgh, financial burdens were weighing him down as he struggled to obtain freelance art projects. He wrote openly to Chrissie, "I asked [God] for patience, and one after another He takes away my prospects of success. . . . He shows me the necessity of long arduous study, and then places circumstances so pressing as to demand immediate money, yet all hopes of money help from the only possible source are dashed to the ground."

Oswald believed his straits may have arisen from his own "ambition and pride," admitting that "the thwarting is good training in patience and consolidation of character." Whatever happened, he planned to maintain trust in God "while He shows me my ignorance, my mistakes, my weaknesses, and takes away all my shallow credulities I used to call faith."

The University of Edinburgh is an ancient institution, already more than three hundred years old when Oswald Chambers enrolled in 1895. He and his fellow learners studied under six separate faculties: Medicine, Science, Law, Divinity, Music, and Art.

30   Oswald Chambers: A Life in Pictures

By the fall of 1896, Chambers was still bereft of money-making opportunities and unable to register for classes. At this point, like softened clay, he was ready to be formed into the vessel God had planned—not a Christian artist but a full-fledged minister of the gospel.

Oswald wrote Chrissie to say he had been in Perth to visit a fellow student's father, "a singular man of deep religious experience, the Holy Spirit being his constant theme of meditation and conversation." The man "astounded" Oswald "by telling me that I *was* to be a minister. He said as soon as I came in with my brother, he felt it impressed on him that I was destined to be a minister, and on leaving he prayed for me most earnestly that God would open my way."

Before long, Oswald was writing, "the thought that is strongest in me is that of entering the ministry.... I cannot keep it hid any longer, for it is perplexing me tremendously. It would be playing with the sacred touch of God to neglect or stifle this strange yet deep conviction that some time I must be a minister."

The King James Version Bible, published in 1900 by Oxford and Cambridge universities, that Oswald Chambers would use in his preaching and teaching.

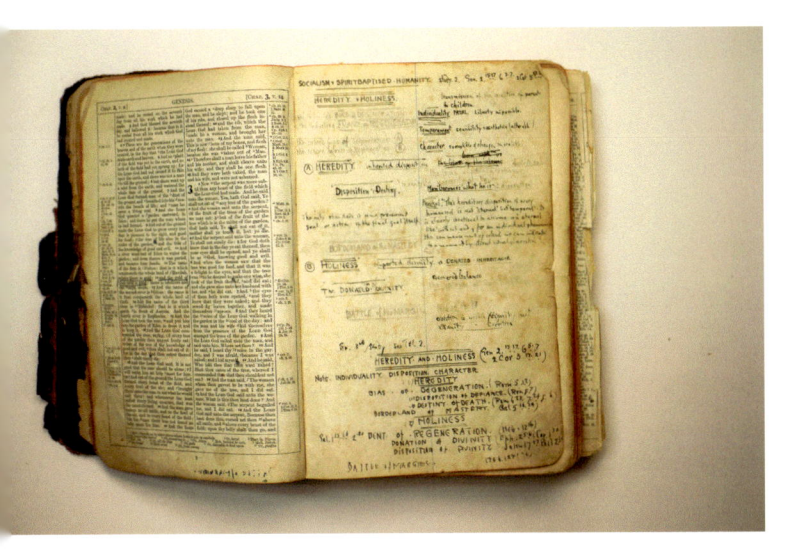

Oswald Chambers in 1915, wearing a clerical collar he never imagined he would wear before the inner struggles of 1896 at Edinburgh University. His friend George Oxer recalled that Chambers had once written, "I shall never go into the ministry until God takes me by the scruff of the neck and throws me in."

The University 31

Oswald Chambers would leave behind thousands of students and the sprawling city-center campus of the University of Edinburgh for about thirty students at Dunoon College, housed in a stately building called Dhalling Mhor.

When he received an unsolicited annual report from a small theological training school in Dunoon, some sixty-five miles west of Edinburgh on Scotland's Firth of Clyde, it seemed a sign. Oswald wrote for more information, learned that the school's leader knew his father, and found he might be able to teach art as he studied theology.

"God moves in a mysterious way," Oswald concluded. "I tremble when I think of what I am going to train for," he wrote to Chrissie. "Pray for me that the Spirit of God will fill me to the drowning of self and the exalting of Jesus."

———◆———

OPPOSITE: Oswald Chambers spent a night on this volcanic hill overlooking the Scottish capital, praying for God's direction in his life. As his brother Franklin reported, "One night alone at Arthur's Seat, Edinburgh, the call of God came with startling suddenness, almost peremptoriness, as a voice actually uttered the words: 'I want you in My service—but I can do without you.' So unmistakable was the call that he responded at once and decided to obey. With no idea of what the next step was to be, he returned to his lodgings and found a report of Dunoon Training College lying on his table."

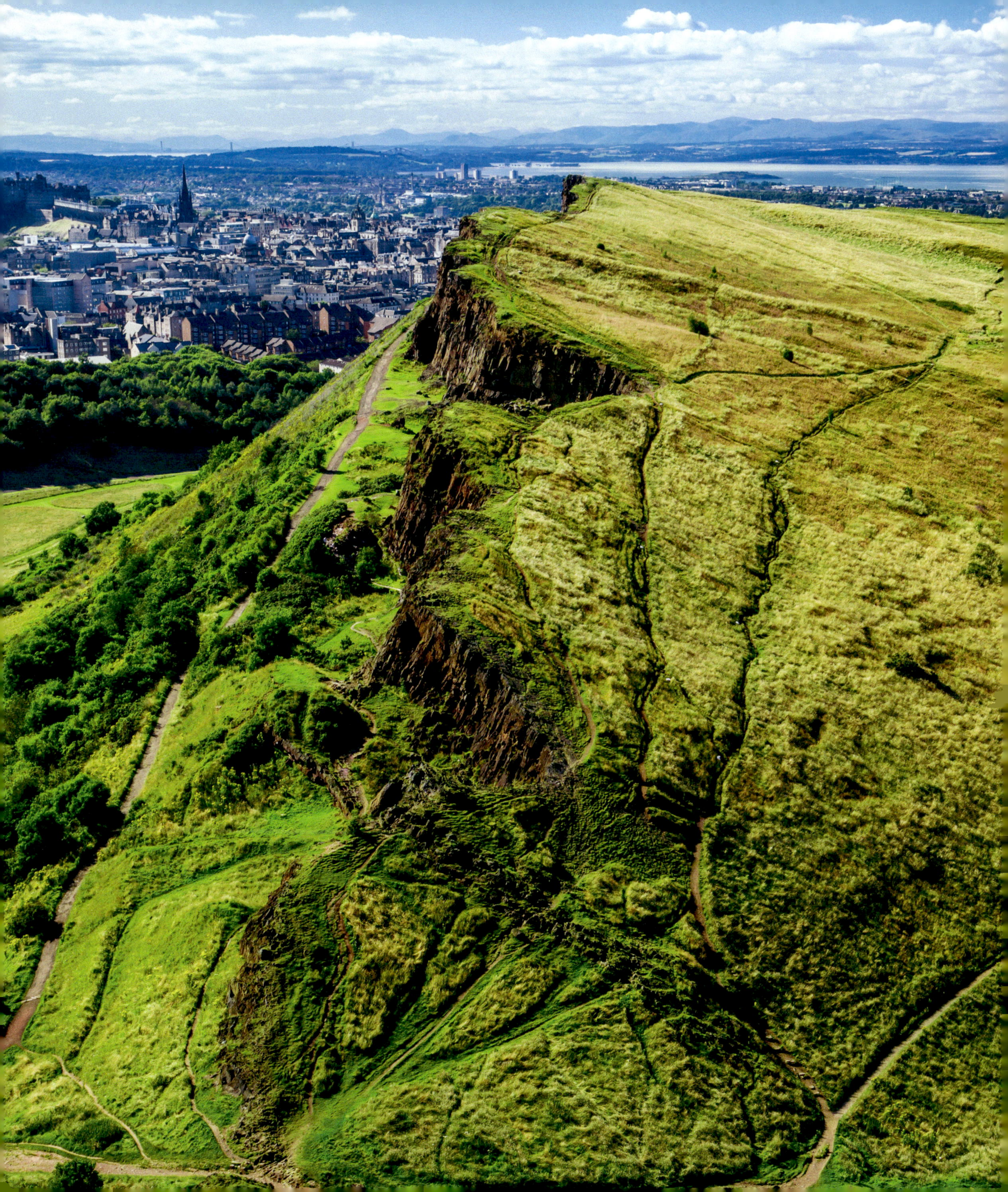

SCENES FROM HIS LIFE

Oswald Chambers's key professors at the University of Edinburgh included Henry Calderwood (left), David Masson (center), and Gerard Baldwin Brown (right).

Calderwood, professor of moral philosophy, was sixty-five years old when Chambers came to Edinburgh; he would die only two years later. Author of the textbook *A Handbook of Moral Philosophy*, he had spoken in the United States in 1880 on the relationship between science and the Bible, in a lecture series organized by telegraph pioneer Samuel F. B. Morse.

Masson, who turned seventy-three in Chambers's first year at the university, taught rhetoric and English literature at Edinburgh. He was known for his six-volume biography of the poet John Milton, and as a literary inspiration of *Peter Pan* author J. M. Barrie.

Brown, called Baldwin rather than Gerard, was only forty-five when Chambers began studying in Edinburgh. An advocate of university education for women (Edinburgh's first female students graduated two years before Oswald enrolled), Baldwin Brown was chair of fine art at the school. Oswald took his course on Classical Archaeology and the History of Ancient Art along with six other students. Brown would later recommend Oswald for an art teaching position at a ladies' college in Edinburgh, though nothing would come of the opportunity.

34   Oswald Chambers: A Life in Pictures

The education Oswald Chambers received in Edinburgh went beyond simply the university setting—his attendance at the Free St. George's Church brought him under the influence of Alexander Whyte (1836–1921), Scotland's leading preacher at the time. Each Sunday evening, after the church service, Whyte would teach some five hundred young men—including Chambers—about the Christian life.

Whyte was difficult to categorize. Called "the last of the Puritans," he was a supporter of D. L. Moody's evangelistic ministry in Scotland. Friendly with the Roman Catholic cardinal John Henry Newman, he taught on Christian mystics such as Thomas à Kempis and Madame Guyon during Chambers's stay in Edinburgh.

As a preacher, Whyte could speak the truth bluntly, a quality Chambers would also develop. In a sermon on prayer, Whyte said,

> *We hate God, indeed, much more than we love ourselves. For we knowingly endanger our immortal souls; every day and every night we risk death and hell itself rather than come close to God and abide in secret prayer. This is the spiritual suicide that we could not have believed possible had we not discovered it in our own atheistical hearts. The thing is far too fearful to put into words. But, put into words for once, this is what our everyday actions say concerning us in this supreme matter of prayer. "No; not tonight," we say, "I do not need to pray tonight. I am really very well tonight. My heart is much steadier in its beats tonight. And, besides, I have business on my hands that will take up all my time tonight."*

People who would later hear Oswald Chambers speak recalled his sometimes "drastic" and "startling" words, spoken not for effect but to make people think. "He seemed to revel in making astounding statements," one man said, "but that was his method of breaking up the ground, as it were, so that he might get in his message."

From a Photo by Elliott & Fry, London.

REV. DR ALEXANDER WHYTE.

The University 35

SCENES FROM HIS LIFE

Princes Street, Edinburgh, around the time Oswald Chambers began university classes less than a mile to the south. Named for the two sons of King George III, Princes Street became the main commercial thoroughfare of Edinburgh. The tower in the background honors Scottish author Sir Walter Scott, who Chambers called "splendidly enjoyable and refreshing." On his 1907 voyage to Japan, Oswald re-read Scott's 1822 novel *The Fortunes of Nigel* and wrote in his diary, "I like him best on second reading of any second-read man." In July 1917, just months before his death, Oswald featured a biography of Scott in the "Books" class he taught to soldiers at the Ezbekieh Gardens in Cairo.

Oswald Chambers read widely and encouraged others to do the same. Major John Skidmore, a friend and coworker in the League of Prayer, once told Oswald that he was struggling to verbalize the spiritual truths he felt in his heart. "Mr. Chambers asked me what I read," Skidmore wrote for the 1933 book *Oswald Chambers: His Life and Work*. "When I told him, nothing but the Bible and books directly associated with it, he diagnosed the difficulty at once and said—'The trouble is you have allowed part of your brain to stagnate for want of use.' Then and there he gave me a list of over fifty books, philosophical, psychological, theological, covering almost every phase of current thought. The outstanding result was a revolution which can only be described as a mental new birth."

In her 2017 book *My Utmost: A Devotional Memoir*, Macy Halford noted Chambers's "habit" of quoting contemporary writers in his teaching. "His favorites included Tennyson, Robert Browning, Henrik Ibsen, and the Scottish fantasy novelist and essayist George MacDonald. Other notable names from the period—like Charles Dickens, George Eliot, Charles Darwin, Friedrich Nietzsche, and Oscar Wilde—showed up, too (if not always favorably)." Oswald Chambers, Halford suggests, was influenced by "a major artistic and literary movement of his day: Realism. Realism was the genre in which many of his literary sources, Christian and otherwise, had written, and their influence on his work had been enormous, even those who, like Ibsen and Eliot, were avowed atheists."

Chambers once called his books "silent, wealthy, loyal lovers . . . friends that are ever true and ever your own."

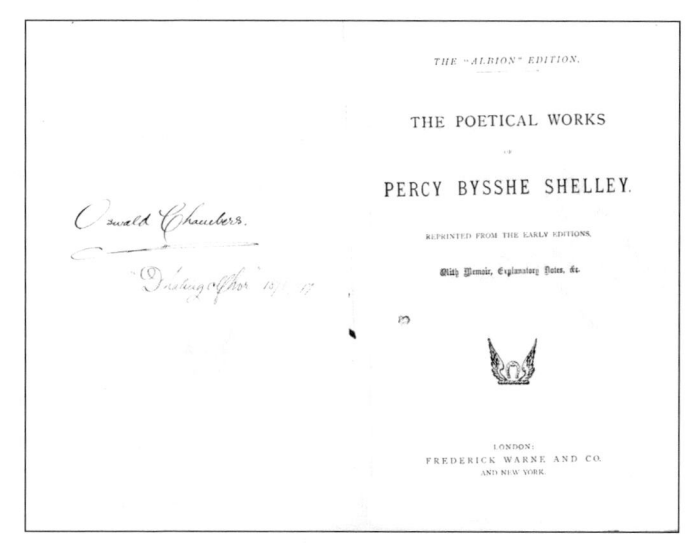

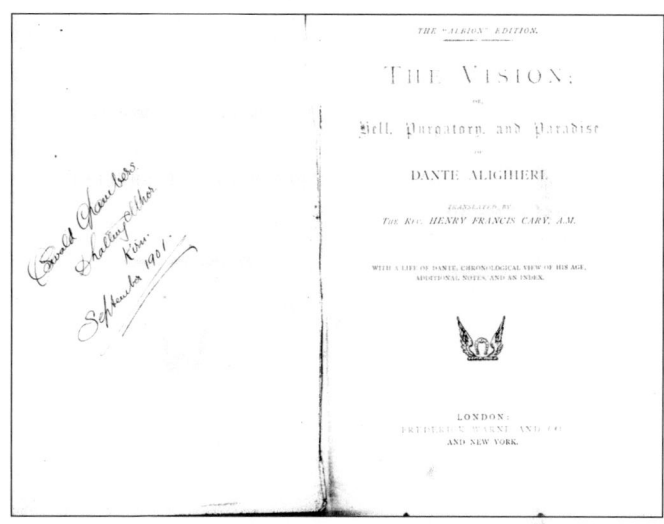

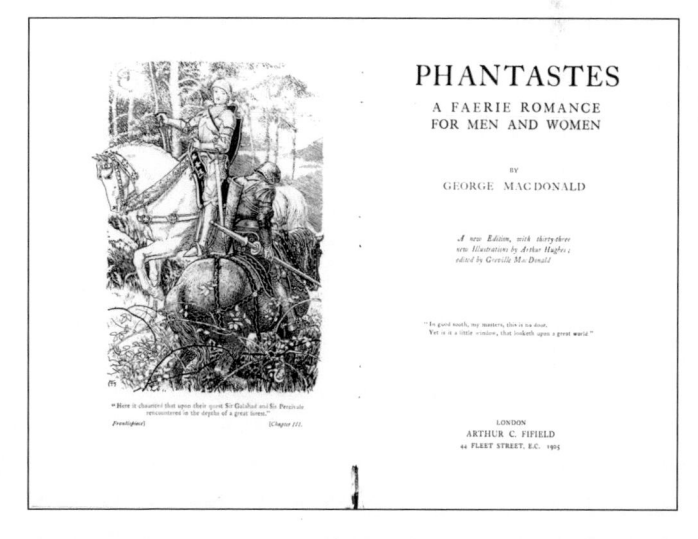

The University 37

This statue of "Highland Mary" Campbell, one-time love of the Scottish poet Robert Burns, was among the sights awaiting Oswald Chambers as he arrived in Dunoon in 1897. The statue had been erected just a year before, for the hundredth anniversary of Burns's death.

4 DUNOON

If Oswald Chambers had been asked which were the most important years in his early life, unquestionably he would have replied, "The years at Dunoon."

BIDDY CHAMBERS, *Oswald Chambers: His Life and Work*

In Dunoon, Scotland, Oswald Chambers would learn—and live—the reality of the apostle Paul's declaration to the believers of Philippi: "I count all things but loss for the excellency of the knowledge of Christ Jesus my Lord: for whom I have suffered the loss of all things, and do count them but dung, that I may win Christ" (Philippians 3:8).

As his wife would later recall, Oswald's years of personal development under Duncan MacGregor, principal of Dunoon College, were vitally important to him. He would gain a spiritual mentor, a father figure seemingly greater than Clarence Chambers himself. But in accepting God's call to Dunoon, Oswald Chambers also gave up his dreams of the art world, and ultimately his long-term relationship with Chrissie Brain. Most difficult of all, in Dunoon Chambers suffered an intense spiritual struggle, a four-year "hell on earth" that nearly drove him mad.

Franklin Chambers recalled that when Oswald, living in Edinburgh, received that unexpected pamphlet from Dunoon College, it had actually been arranged by their father. The elder Chambers "was delighted" when his son announced plans to apply for the school.

Others were less enthused. On February 15, 1897, the day before he left the Scottish capital, Oswald wrote in his diary, "I have no doubt I am doing the right thing in going to Dunoon, and the next five years by the grace of God will silence the careful misgivings of my considerate friends and relatives."

Oswald's experience with MacGregor, a man twenty-five years his senior, quickly confirmed his expectations. "I look upon him as a re-incarnation of Jesus Christ by His Spirit, so like is he to his Master," Oswald wrote to a friend. "I never loved a man as I love him." Pastor of the Dunoon Baptist Church, MacGregor started his college to correct what he saw as deficiencies in the preparation of men for the ministry. He preferred to combine his classroom teaching with a residential presence in the students' lives, a philosophy Oswald Chambers embraced and later employed in his own ministry.

Duncan MacGregor's son, Esdaile, called Oswald "the most striking personality we had ever had as a student," a young man of remarkable thinness and surprisingly long hair, "two things which made him a figure to be noted wherever he went." And Chambers went many places, teaching private art classes, starting a Robert Browning poetry society, attending meetings of the Baptist church, even filling pulpits for other churches.

The Rev. and Mrs. Duncan MacGregor, surrounded by students at Dunoon College in the years after Oswald attended. "How can Oswald Chambers be condensed into anything like a readable reminiscence?" Mrs. MacGregor wrote after his death. "There is no label that one can attach to him and be satisfied—artist, poet, philosopher, preacher and teacher, comedian—for he had a delicious sense of humour and dramatic power, if he cared to use it."

Chambers's eager, youthful preaching style, however, was not universally appreciated. As Esdaile MacGregor recalled, "he seemed to create a fear of God rather than of confidence and love"—and one church, which had asked Duncan MacGregor for help with pulpit supply, specified that it did *not* want the "lang-haired swearin' parson."

By the fall of 1898, Chambers had become a tutor in the college, teaching logic, psychology, and moral philosophy, and even creating his own textbook, *Outlines for the Study of Historical Philosophy*, two years later. Though quite young himself—he was only twenty-four when he began teaching—Oswald enjoyed working with students, "over whom he had a great and lasting influence for good," in Esdaile's words. But the younger MacGregor also recalled a less agreeable job for Oswald Chambers—serving as deacon in the Dunoon Baptist Church: "He found that he had little in common with the older men of fixed habits and fixed beliefs."

College had started well, and Oswald wrote to Chrissie in September 1897, "I have great hopes for it, it is on the right lines." He found a ministerial soulmate in Duncan MacGregor, believing him one of the greatest men of God he had ever met; Esdaile remembered that "my father reciprocated the admiration." And in Dunoon, under Duncan MacGregor's leadership, Oswald Chambers interacted with other godly men who challenged him in faith and ministry.

Oswald Chambers in his early twenties. A niece, Irene, described his "thin, gaunt face and piercing grey-blue eyes," but said visits from "Uncle Oswald" were always accompanied by laughter, fun, and pranks. Years later, after Oswald's death, Irene would recall a man "quite without any suggestion of moral superiority," saying, "He was a total abstainer and he hated smoking and card playing, yet I have known him to be in the company of folk who were smoking and playing cards, and while refusing to take part, yet create no sense of discomfort."

Dunoon 41

Key influences included Dr. Alexander Whyte, whose church Oswald had attended in Edinburgh; Rev. Dinsdale Young of Edinburgh, "who seemed to persuade him," as Esdaile recalled, "that there was work for him in preaching a simpler and friendlier gospel"; and the internationally known, London-based Baptist pastor F. B. Meyer, whose presentation on the Holy Spirit sparked Oswald's great crisis of life.

Frederick Brotherton Meyer (1847–1929) was pastoring London's Christ Church when he visited Dunoon and spoke on the Holy Spirit. Meyer's talk set Oswald Chambers on a long, painful path to "entire consecration."

"After I was born again as a lad I enjoyed the presence of Jesus Christ wonderfully," he would later state in a public testimony. But after Meyer spoke on God's Spirit, "I determined to have all that was going and went to my room and asked God simply and definitely for the baptism of the Holy Spirit, whatever that meant. From that day on for four years, nothing but the overruling grace of God and the kindness of friends kept me out of an asylum."

God seemed to answer Oswald's prayer with only an increasingly clear view of his failure and sin. During his years of struggle, he was ordained to the ministry, preached often, and even managed the college after Duncan MacGregor was seriously injured in a fall from the roof. Many spoke well of Chambers, but he battled deep feelings of unworthiness. "I am . . . thought a great deal more highly of than I deserve," he wrote his father in September 1901. "I am neither great nor good nor noble, nor do I think I am."

A year earlier, he had cried out in a poem,

Cowardly sorrow maketh plaint,
"This is hard to bear."
Makes a shape at being saint,
While the loathsome sin doth taint
All that others think so fair.

OPPOSITE: The "devotional hut" in Zeitoun, Egypt, where Oswald Chambers would minister to soldiers during World War I. The signs on the side and back walls quote Romans 5:8 and 9. In the main Y.M.C.A. hut, as an Australian soldier recalled, Chambers had posted a "huge" placard of the life-changing Luke 11:13 on the front wall, behind the platform from which he spoke.

42   Oswald Chambers: A Life in Pictures

In the final few months of his battle, Oswald admitted he was "getting very desperate," saying, "I knew that if what I had was all the Christianity there was, the thing was a fraud." But God placed a verse in Chambers's mind, one that would become key to his entire ministry: "If ye then, being evil, know how to give good gifts unto your children; how much more shall your heavenly Father give the Holy Spirit to them that ask him?" (Luke 11:13).

During a mission meeting held in Dunoon, Chambers stood to publicly admit his need, only to hear the leader tell the assembly that Oswald had risen to set an example for everyone else. "Up I got again," Chambers recalled, "and said, 'I got up for no one's sake, I got up for my own sake. . . .' And then and there I claimed the gift of the Holy Spirit in dogged committal on Luke 11:13."

Even then, there were no miraculous changes, "no vision of heaven or of angels," as Oswald would say. But shortly afterward, having been asked to speak at a meeting, forty people responded to his gospel presentation. "Did I praise God?" Oswald asked. "No, I was terrified, and left them to the workers." He went quickly to Duncan MacGregor, who suggested that the effect of his preaching that night was "power from on high" in answer to Oswald's claiming of the Holy Spirit.

Immediately, Chambers realized his mistake—he had been basing his spiritual well-being on his own sacrifice rather than the Lord's immense love. "Glory be to God," he said later,

> *the last aching abyss of the human heart is filled to overflowing with the love of God. . . .*

When you know what God has done for you the power and the tyranny of sin is gone, and the radiant, unspeakable emancipation of the indwelling Christ has come, and when you see men and women who should be princes and princesses with God bound up in a show of things—oh, you begin to understand what the Apostle meant when he said he wished that he himself were accursed from Christ that men might be saved!

"If the previous years had been hell on earth," Oswald would say, the years since his entire consecration had "truly been heaven on earth." Freed from his burden, he would follow God's leading and represent heaven to the far reaches of earth.

At Dunoon, Oswald had become involved with the interdenominational Pentecostal League of Prayer, through which he met Japanese evangelist Juji Nakada. A camaraderie quickly developed, and they made plans for a preaching and teaching tour of America and Japan.

Oswald left Dunoon after not quite a decade as student, coworker, and friend of Duncan MacGregor. Though "he goes to the foreign field, as he believes, in answer to a clear call from God, and will be followed with our earnest prayers and deep affection," the principal wrote in the college's annual report for 1906, "we regard the absence of Mr. Chambers as an unspeakable loss."

Dunoon's loss would prove to be the larger Christian world's gain.

SCENES FROM HIS LIFE

Of Duncan MacGregor, Oswald Chambers wrote to a friend, "I wish you knew him—character, character, character! To the backbone, noble, unselfish, and holy."

A Baptist pastor who'd led churches in England, Wales, and Chicago, Illinois, MacGregor returned to his native Scotland in 1885 to pastor the Dunoon Baptist Church. After a few years, he began to train young men for the ministry, with Dunoon College meeting in the MacGregor family home, called Dhalling Mhor. Oswald Chambers would leave Edinburgh for Dunoon in early 1897, both to study and serve as tutor to fellow students.

Like Alexander Whyte in Edinburgh, Duncan MacGregor was unconfined by the expectations of others. While deeply involved in the Baptist denomination, his college was interdenominational. A supporter of Scotland's crofters (tenant farmers), he publicly campaigned for a likeminded Catholic candidate in a Parliamentary election. In 1901, he published a novel called *Lady Christ*, a title that could "astonish a modern reviewer," according to *The Bookseller*, a monthly newspaper of British literature.

But Oswald perceived no contentiousness in MacGregor's ways, saying, "I never knew him in a controversy in my life."

Duncan MacGregor and Dunoon Baptist Church

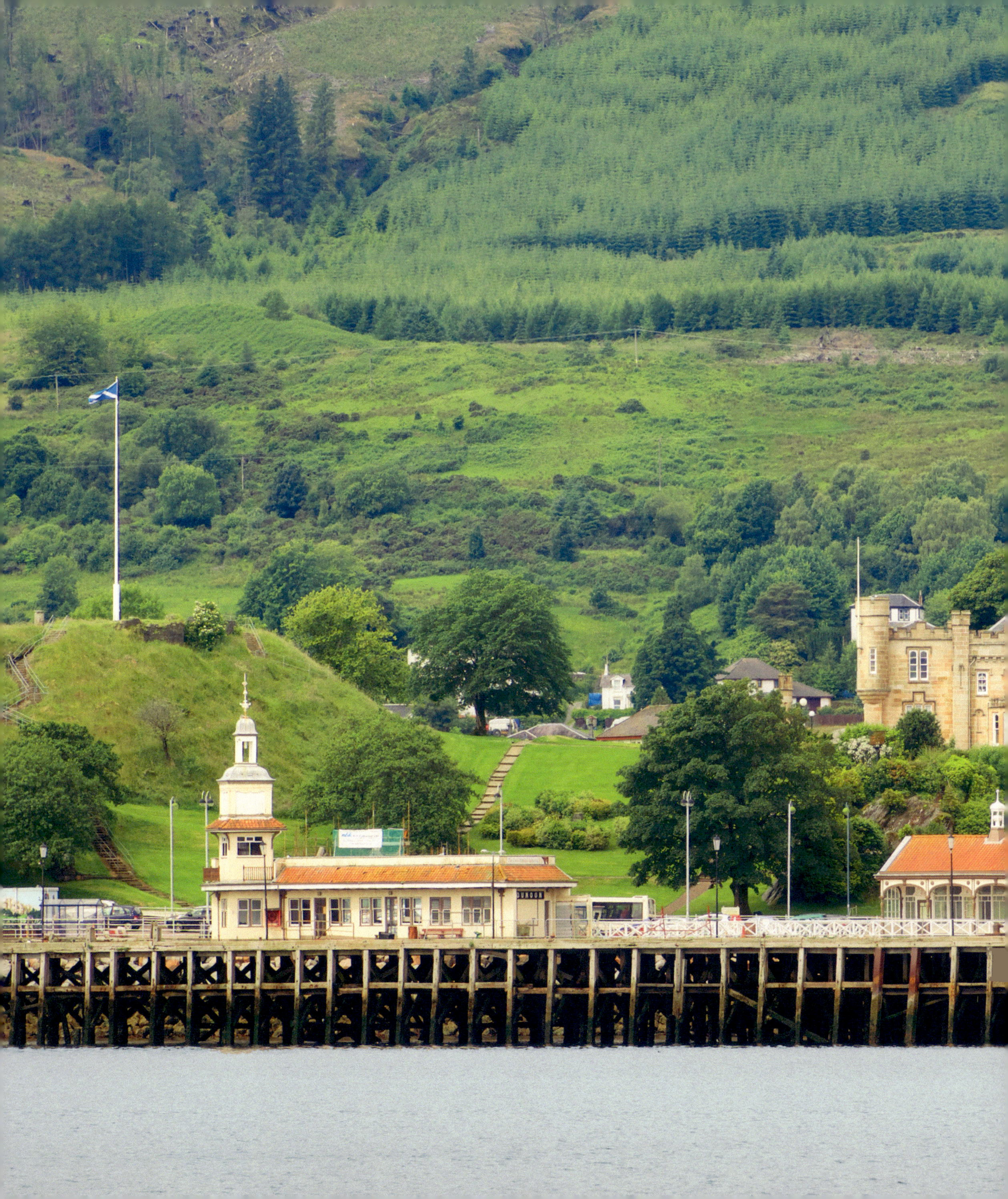
DUNOON

The Dunoon pier, where Oswald Chambers arrived in and departed from the town. He quickly involved himself in community life, managing Duncan MacGregor's campaign for a school board seat, starting a Robert Browning poetry society, and writing for the local newspaper, *The Dunoon Herald*. "He became marked also," Esdaile MacGregor recalled, "for his love of walks among the hills, with his dog, Tweed."

While at Dunoon College, Oswald Chambers saw trust in God exemplified by William Quarrier, founder of the Bridge of Weir Orphan Homes, a self-contained village of forty-plus cottages located twenty miles southeast of Dunoon. It was Quarrier, Franklin Chambers recalled, "who taught Oswald the genuine, childlike simplicity of prayer, the prayer that never doubts or questions, or debates the possibility of an answer. Oswald used to tell how often on a Friday night he and this man of God would kneel in prayer, and Quarrier would quietly and simply tell his Father that he needed over £700 next week 'for these bairns of Yours,' and leave the matter there and never trouble. And the money came in, as it does to this day—no advertising, no wire-pulling, only importunate prayer."

SCENES FROM HIS LIFE

An undated photo of children from Quarrier's village. During his ministry, Oswald Chambers would teach that care for the needy does not spring from our love for them—"the fundamental fact," he said, "is that supreme love for our Lord alone gives us the motive power of service to any extent for others." Franklin Chambers recalled a time when his brother gave everything he had to a drunken beggar. "Taking him under a lamp," Franklin wrote, "he heard his story and being a quick judge of character, he said, 'Man, I believe your story is all lies, but my Master tells me to give to everyone that asks, so there is my last shilling.' As he gave it him he said, 'I thought it was a shilling but it is half a crown [worth about two and a half times the shilling]. There you are, the Lord bless you.' . . . He frequently said he believed beggars were sent to test one's obedience of faith." Chambers's first biographer, D. W. Lambert, told of a similar incident: "I remember at Perth Convention seeing him talking to a man, obviously a scrounger, and coming away after handing him something. 'Yes,' he said, 'I gave him a shilling and told him he did not deserve it, but I gave because my Master commanded me to, and if he went and damned himself with it, it was not my concern.'"

SCENES FROM HIS LIFE

By age twenty-four, Oswald Chambers was tutoring Dunoon College students in logic, psychology, and moral philosophy, "subjects in which he had received some instruction in Edinburgh, but which he got up chiefly in private study," Esdaile MacGregor reported. Within two years, Oswald had created his own twenty-page, twenty-four lesson booklet titled *Outlines for the Study of Historical Philosophy*, covering ancient, pre-Socratic philosophy through the ideologies of Chambers's time, including "Evolutional Ethics" with "Darwinianism as the starting point." Charles Darwin, who had studied medicine at the University of Edinburgh before postulating the evolutionary theories that made him famous, had died less than two decades before.

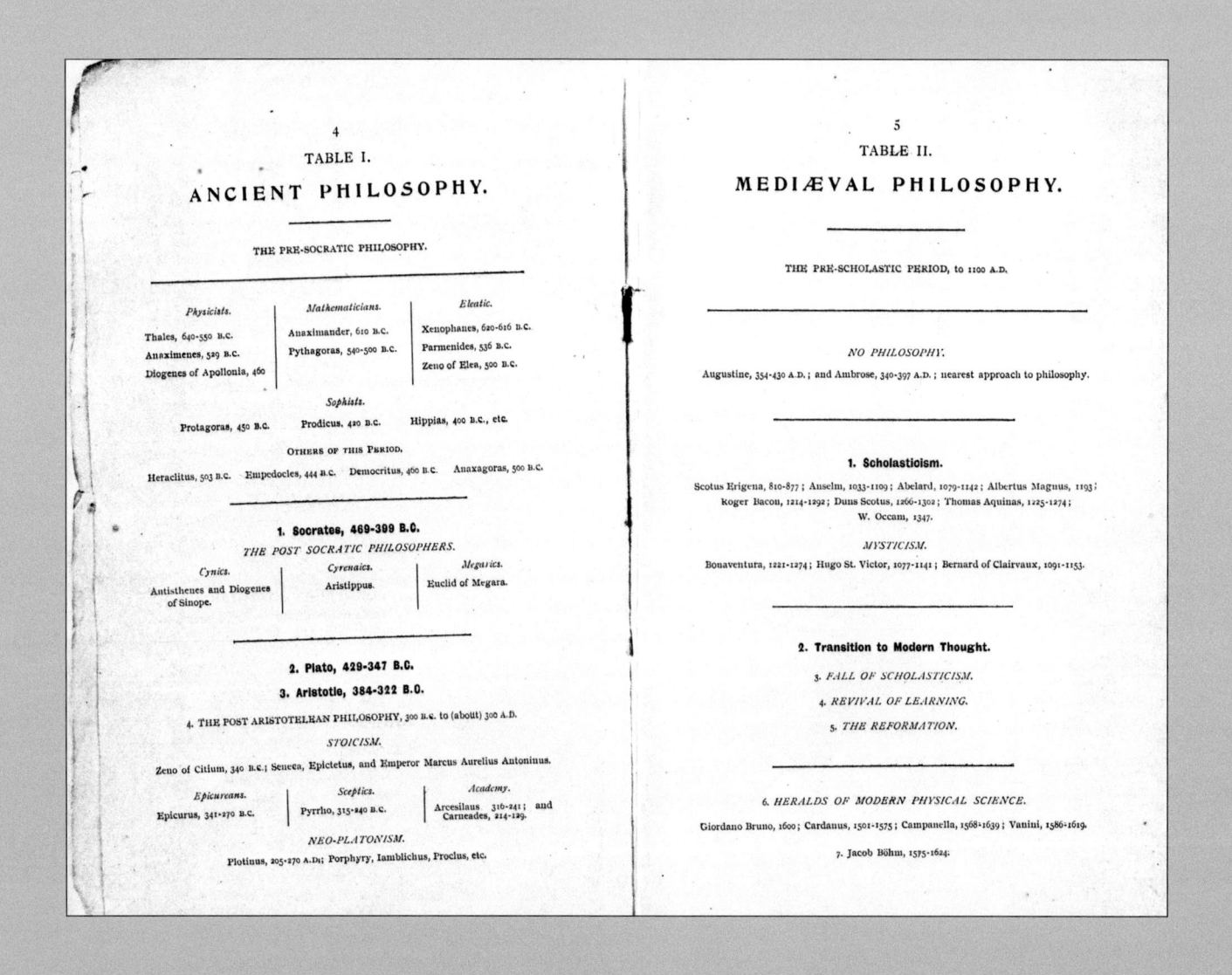

Sometime during his Dunoon years, Oswald Chambers posed for this portrait with two of his three brothers—Franklin (left) and Ernest (right).

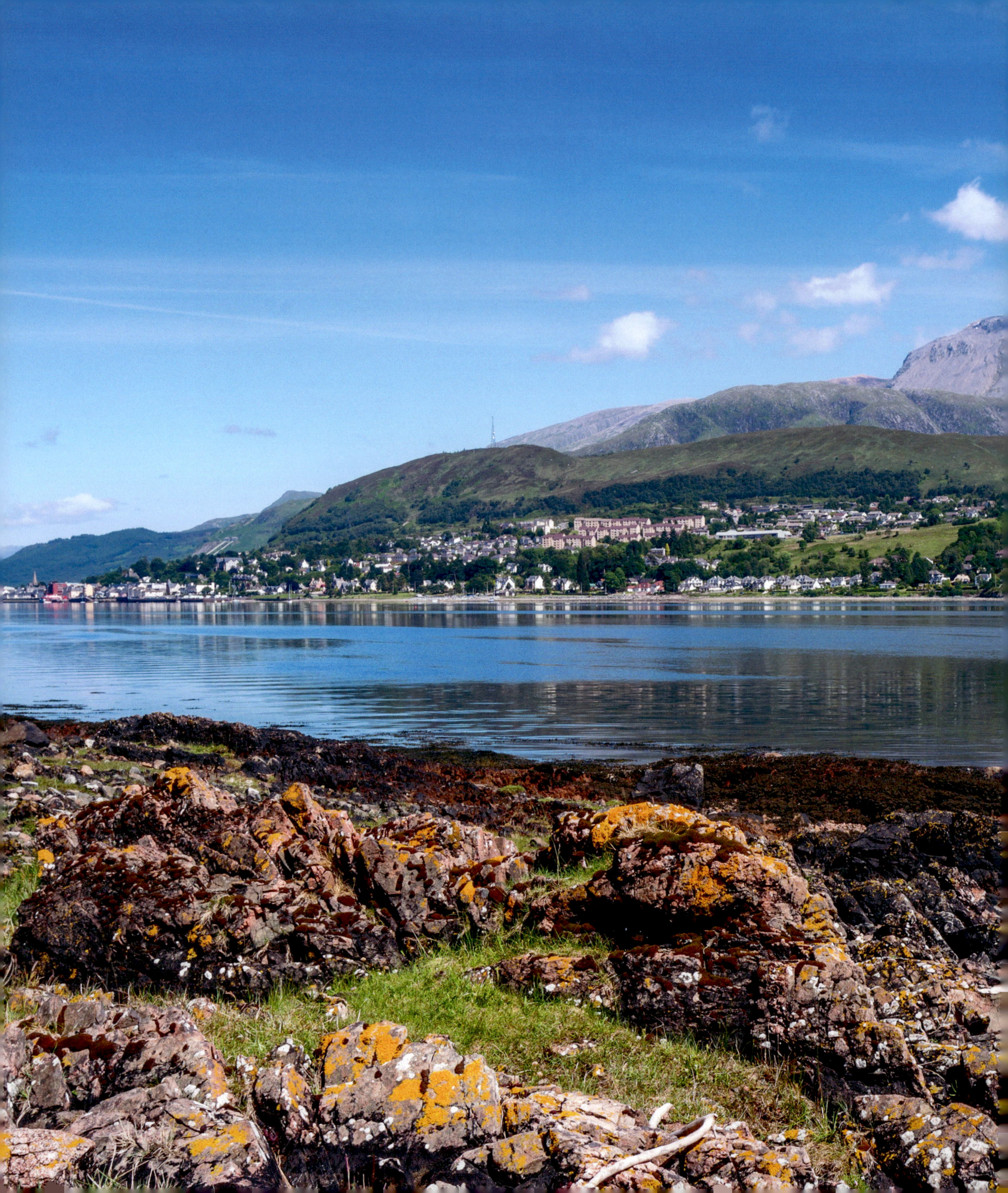

Scotland's Ben Nevis, the tallest mountain in the British Isles at 4,400 feet (1,345 meters), was a favorite escape for Oswald Chambers. About 60 miles north of Dunoon as the crow flies, it towered over the home of a bachelor shepherd, John Cameron, from whom Chambers learned much of prayer. "Few knew him, but I knew him," Oswald wrote to his brother and sister-in-law, Franklin and Ethel, in 1907. "I remember him on his death-bed in his home on the slopes of Ben Nevis, he could not speak but held out his arms and I bent down and kissed him. The snows were deep not only around him, but on his own head. A stern mountain crag, but the heart of a moss rose was his. If anyone has felt the tenderness of a rugged old Highlander's embrace and love, they'll know why I thank my God upon my remembrances of old John Cameron. How he knew God! How he talked with God! And how he taught me out on those hills—at midnight, at dawn-light, and at noonday have I knelt before that old veteran in prayer. Truly it was a great goodness of God to allow me to know such men."

Beyond the influence of the old man himself, Oswald Chambers learned from his work. "I did not like it at the time, but I am thankful now I had to do shepherding in the Highlands of Scotland," he would say. "When you have to carry across your shoulders a dirty old wether [a castrated ram] and bring it down the mountain side you will soon know whether it is not the most taxing, the most exhausting, and the most exasperating work; and Jesus uses this as an illustration of a passion for souls."

SCENES FROM HIS LIFE

Two of Oswald Chambers's artistic creations indicate the inner stress of his long spiritual crisis at Dunoon—an undated sketch of a stormy sea, and the handwritten text of his poem "Prayer Pleading," dated September 30, 1901, as the struggle reached its breaking point. Oswald actually completed two poems that day, the second titled "Fruitless Sorrow":

I would rather the flood went o'er me,
 The flood of the great wild sea,
With its acres of secret waters
 Than mourn o'er the never-to-be.

Oh, the wounds of the martyred Master
 Are sweet to my mind of grief,
I would leap with joy at disaster,
 Akin to the crucified thief.

But the sapping of hopeless sorrow
    Means death to a youthful life,
But the pain of each new day's morrow
    Serves as good to the new day's strife.

In "Prayer Pleading," Chambers begged God, "O do hear me, O do hear me / Else I think my heart will break," crying out for "a living touch with Thee." The poem ends,

    O Lord Jesus, hear my crying
        For a consecrated life.
    For I bite the dust in trying
        For release from this dark strife.

Dunoon

SCENES FROM HIS LIFE

A month after "Prayer Pleading," the storm finally ended, as suggested by the sketch of a peaceful harbor from this time, and the serene portrait of a thirty-year-old Oswald Chambers three years later. In 1906, looking back from the perspective of five years, Oswald appended a victorious note to his plaintive poem: "In November 1901 by an entire consecration and acceptance of sanctification at the Lord's hands, I was baptized with the Holy Ghost, and unspeakable joy and peace have resulted, ever-deepening since."

Major John Skidmore, who later worked with Oswald in the League of Prayer, recalled him saying, "The baptism of the Holy Ghost does not make you think of time or eternity, it is one amazing, glorious *now*." Chambers also told Skidmore, "It is no wonder that I talk so much about altered disposition: God altered mine; I was there when He did it, and I have been there ever since."

56   Oswald Chambers: A Life in Pictures

Dunoon 57

Oswald Chambers spent about eight months in the United States during a long trip that began in November 1906. The following May, in North Carolina for outdoor Bible meetings, he wrote to his sister Edith, "This place is a veritable Garden of Eden for beauty. Right on the top of the mountains with an inimitable view, surrounded by grand and lofty oaks and pine trees, with the great rolling river at your feet in the valley and a vast space of heaven." Even better was the people's craving for Scripture: "I go on talking to them out of the Bible for hours at a stretch."

5 "ROUND THE WORLD ALL RIGHT"

He told me he was going round the world one day—a very alluring idea to entertain I used to think, but unlikely to happen! But Chambers went round the world all right.

REV. THOMAS HOUSTON, *Oswald Chambers: His Life and Work*

Oswald Chambers's creative talents were so impressive, as his brother Franklin said, "it seemed that his future in the art world was assured." His native intelligence and teaching ability might have led him to the faculty of a large university. But his love for Christ sent him to country churches, city missions, and outdoor camp meetings to reach average, everyday people, those he described as "hungry for God."

He would expand his personal and ministry horizons with an around-the-world trip from early November 1906 through late August 1907, a journey that introduced him to a broad spectrum of people in the United States—including African-Americans, Native Americans, Quakers, and the often exuberant participants of Holiness Movement revivals.

Oswald would also spend time in Japan, homeland of his newfound friend and ministry partner Juji Nakada. In both North America and Asia, and at points in between, Chambers drank in unforgettable sights from the decks of ships, railroad car berths, horse-drawn carriages and sleighs, and wherever his own legs took him.

Since the late spring, Chambers and Nakada had spoken in churches and conferences throughout England and Scotland. Both men had made a strong impression. A resident of a small Yorkshire town recalled, "Looking over the village as they walked from the station, the tall Scotsman drew himself up and turning to his short, vivacious companion said, 'Brother Nakada, we put our feet down in Denby Dale for Christ.' And so it proved."

But the larger world beckoned. "I know in my bones that it is 'Go ye into all the world and make disciples of all the nations,'" Oswald would write to Franklin. Accordingly, he and Nakada booked passage for a nine-day crossing to the United States.

Ten years earlier, Nakada had studied at the Moody Bible Institute in Chicago. He also had connections with a Cincinnati college called God's Bible School. Once in North America, Nakada and Chambers spent several weeks with various believers in the east, "being handed around through these States in a wonderful way," as Oswald would describe it, before departing for a conference at the Cincinnati school. After that, he was asked to serve on its faculty for a few months.

The iconic image of Oswald Chambers, bound for America and Japan in 1906.

Oswald Chambers arrived in Cincinnati on December 21, 1906, finding an institution high on a hill dubbed the "Mount of Blessings." With classroom space, a print shop, a rescue home, and an orphanage, God's Bible School was "all run on faith lines," like Dunoon had been. Chambers agreed to stay until July, teaching and writing—and mulling the possibilities of more such schools. "My heart swells," he said, "at the big thoughts and visions that come of founding Bible schools on these holiness lines in Britain and different parts of the world."

While Cincinnati became Chambers's home base, his travels also took him to Columbus, Ohio; Cambridge Springs, Pennsylvania; Providence, Rhode Island; Asheville, North Carolina; and Niagara Falls, New York. His visit to the latter included an invitation to speak at a Baptist church on a reservation, where "an old Indian chief will interpret," he wrote his sister Florence. "What ceaseless and amazing interests pack my life!"

Chambers had particularly enjoyed his time in Newport, Rhode Island, with a family of Quakers and Sophie, the "saved and sanctified" African-American who lived with them. "These black people are gems," he wrote. "They laugh and shout 'Glory!' and interrupt the preacher to tell the audience an incident they think illustrates the point—gloriously unconventional."

God's Bible School was only six years old when Oswald Chambers visited for the first time. Founded by Methodist minister Martin Wells Knapp, the institution was part of the "Holiness Movement," a multidenominational, grassroots initiative calling Christians to the doctrines of regeneration and entire sanctification as taught by Methodism's founder, John Wesley.

"Round the World All Right"

A "picketer" from God's Bible School, displaying Scripture on the streets of Cincinnati.

This "American way" often took Chambers by surprise. In March, as he walked down a Cincinnati street with the Rev. Arthur Greene (pictured on page 91), his companion suddenly shouted, "I hate the devil!" Oswald shouted in return, "So do I!" At that moment, Chambers reported, a passerby with tears in his eyes approached the two men to ask about the way of salvation. "Oh," Chambers wrote to his brother Ernest, "these delightful unconventional ways suit me down to the ground!"

By early April, Chambers was writing to Florence that the Cincinnatians were "very open-minded and teachable," lacking the theological prejudices and preconceived notions of people in Great Britain. "In the homeland I continually heard—'Don't preach like that, people won't understand you.' Here I find them very teachable and mouldable, and my responsibility is increased for they take what I say as of lasting authority." Soon, Oswald would find a similar response among a very different people, the Japanese.

After a ten-day camp meeting in Cincinnati in early June, Oswald got on a train for Seattle, where he would rejoin Nakada, board the *Empress of Japan*, and sail across the Pacific. The sixteen-day journey, which encompassed Chambers's thirty-third birthday, ended in Yokohama, one of the first Japanese ports opened to foreign trade less than fifty years earlier.

OPPOSITE: Mount Fuji looms over modern Yokohama, the city that in 1907 introduced Oswald Chambers to Juji Nakada's homeland. "Three days in Japan!" Oswald wrote in his diary. "It is exceedingly difficult to realize that it is all *real*. You feel continually as if you must soon wake up to the stern realities of daily life. But no, the 'Earl's Court Exhibition' goes on, not only all round you but to your very mouth in tea and food."

62   Oswald Chambers: A Life in Pictures

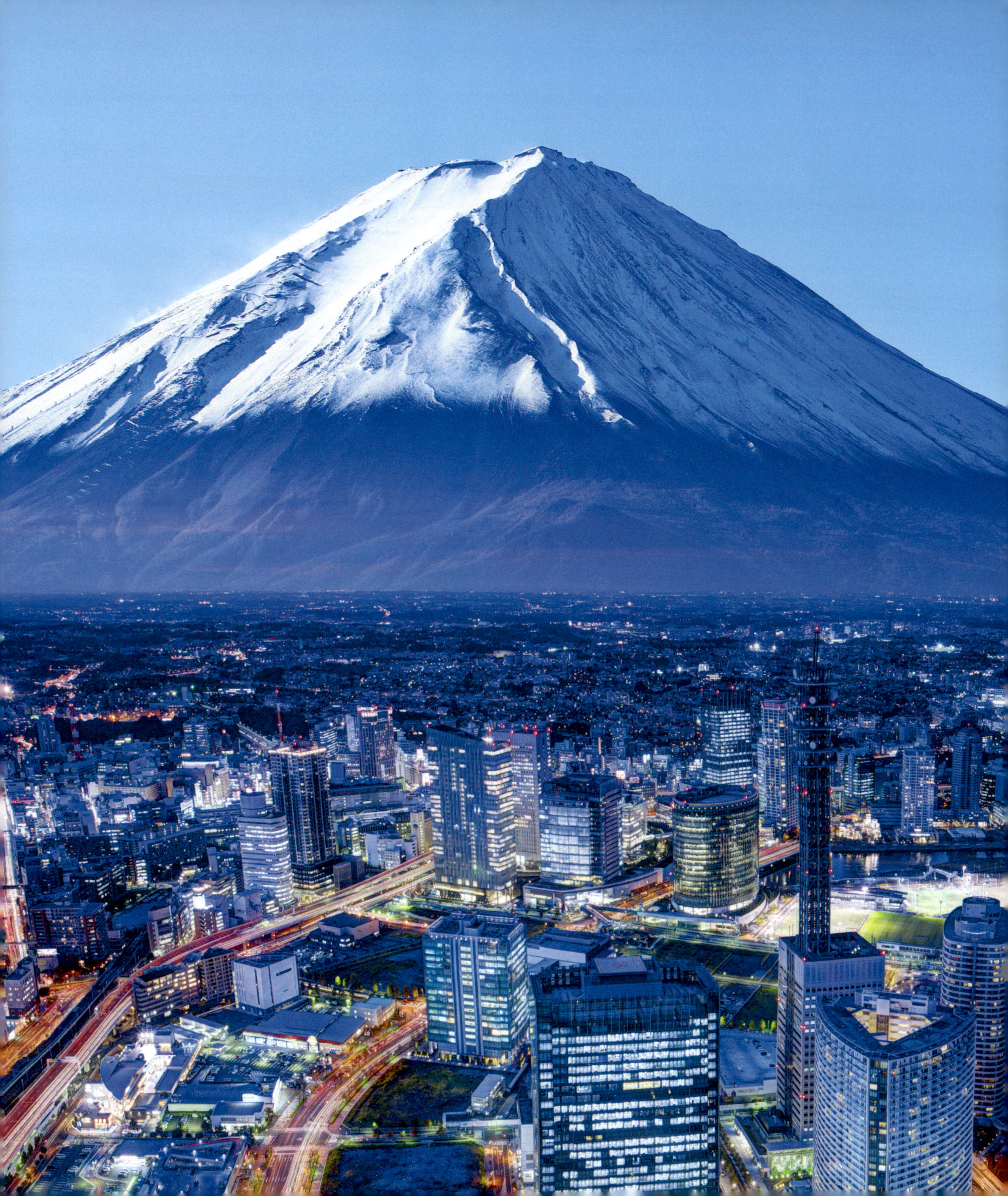

This map of Japan was printed in 1900, seven years before Oswald Chambers visited. He spent about a month in Japan, thoroughly mesmerized by the country and its people. "The whole thing has so absorbed and enthralled me that I have been like the Queen of Sheba," he wrote in his diary. Key stops included:

1 **YOKOHAMA:** Port city on Tokyo Bay, Oswald's point of arrival on July 27, 1907.

2 **TOKYO:** National capital, site of the Oriental Mission Society Bible School, Oswald's home base in Japan. He would also spend time at the Tokyo Y.M.C.A. before visiting other cities, returning to Tokyo for about half of August.

3 **KARUIZAWA:** Mountain resort town where Oswald Chambers and Juji Nakada attended a missionary conference on August 6, 1907.

4 **NAGASAKI:** Port city of southwestern Japan, on the South China Sea. Chambers arrived here on August 7, 1907, to hold an evening meeting. "Nakada tells me it is the hardest place in Japan, being a seaport," Oswald wrote in his diary. "It is very godless, but they all seem eager to listen."

5 **KOBE:** Port city on Osaka Bay, from which Oswald Chambers departed Japan on August 26, 1907. He would sail through the Inland Sea, "without doubt the most lovely place I was ever in," on the way to Shanghai, China, first stop on a six-week journey home.

Within days of their July 27 arrival, Chambers and Nakada were holding evangelistic services around Tokyo, attending a missionary conference in Karuizawa, and preaching in Nagasaki. Oswald was smitten by Japan and its people. "This is certainly the most entrancing country I could conceive possible. The whole thing has so absorbed and enthralled me that I have been like the Queen of Sheba," he wrote in his diary.

The Japanese, Oswald wrote to his brother Franklin, "simply swallow salvation wholesale. I never imagined or saw anything quite like it." Nakada, he reported, was a mighty preacher among his own people. "They come out fifty to a hundred, without any persuasion, and then the work begins. Every worker gets on his knees with his Bible and instruction goes on for hours, for they know nothing of the Christian revelation; they will stay all night, and when they do get through it is wonderful. God puts His seal on these people as He rarely seems to do in the homeland or America."

All too soon, Chambers had to leave the "sort of Alice in Wonderland place" to return to England. He boarded the S.S. *Bingo Maru* on August 22, with an itinerary including Kobe, Shanghai, Hong Kong, Singapore, Colombo, the Red Sea, the Suez Canal, Port Said, and the Mediterranean. From Marseilles, on October 10, he wrote, "Here ends this most profitable voyage, as an education very difficult to estimate. I hope to reap benefits therefrom all my after life, however long or short."

Japanese evangelist Juji Nakada traveled vast distances with Oswald Chambers, observing him in private as well as public settings. Nakada recalled Oswald lying in his ship's berth amid rough seas, praying for others. "He turned the leaves of his book which contained the names of those to be prayed for," he wrote after Oswald's death, "and day or night he never ceased praying and interceding for them, even though at times he did not feel too good."

Earlier dreams of a career in art, of a life in the cultured world of music and paintings and poetry, were now a rapidly receding memory for Oswald Chambers. His friend Thomas Houston had noticed the change beginning in their later years at Dunoon, as Oswald "appeared to make less of self-culture as a pursuit than in the earlier years; yet then perhaps more than ever his personal culture was developing and maturing, for with him it seemed more and more to be derived from living for others and seeking to bring men to Him Who is the Source of all light and life, Our Lord Jesus Christ."

Now, as he entered what would be the final decade of his life, Oswald devoted himself to the work of the League of Prayer—and discovered the earthly love of his life.

SCENES FROM HIS LIFE

Another portrait of Oswald Chambers, taken as he sailed to the United States for the first time. Chambers and his fellow minister, Juji Nakada, traveled aboard a ship called the *Baltic*, which apparently enjoyed divine protection on its passage from Liverpool to New York. "Probably the most persistent sentiment with me is the watch of the angel hosts in answer to the prayers of the numerous saints in the homeland," Chambers wrote five days into the journey. "It seems to me as if a special watch surrounded this boat, I seem to hear them in the rolling air and to feel their touches even through my whole body."

He would return to that same theme in Egypt, as he noted in his diary on December 3, 1915: "As I walked through the lines to-night, alone in this mighty desert, under the serene dome of sky and the wonderful stars, I realized again the unique sense of the presence of angels. I noticed it repeatedly the first time I went abroad. It is quite distinct from the certainty that God is guarding, this is the beautiful sense of angel presence. Anyway that is how it strikes me and I thank God for it."

"Round the World All Right"   67

SCENES FROM HIS LIFE

Oswald Chambers was one of the "other," unnamed workers referenced in an advertisement for the 1906 Christmas convention at God's Bible School in Cincinnati. Juji Nakada, who introduced Oswald to the school's leadership, later wrote that he "delivered wonderful Bible lessons which stirred and enlivened the Holiness folks as well as the students. Thus he became intimately acquainted with the Holiness work and people of America, and afterward made many trips back to this land to preach and teach at Cincinnati Bible School."

God's Bible School and Missionary Training Home
CHRISTMAS CONVENTION,
December 21-30, 1906,
AT GOD'S BIBLE SCHOOL AND GOD'S BIBLE SCHOOL GEORGE STREET MISSION, CINCINNATI, OHIO.

Meetings at "Mount of Blessings" every day at 10:30 A. M. and 2:30 P. M., and at George Street Mission every night at 7:30 o'clock.

FATHER, SON AND HOLY GHOST IN CHARGE.

WORKERS:—George B. Kulp, L. B. Compton, E. A. Fergerson, Arthur Green, Lew A. Standley, M. G. Standley, and Brother Nakada, Brother and Sister Cowman's co-worker in Japan, Fred T. Fuge, and others.

With the start of the new year, "Brother Chambers" filled a faculty role at God's Bible School. "For many months they have been praying for a teacher, and at their request I have agreed to stay until July and teach and write some books," he wrote to his sister Florence. He is shown here (below) with several students.

Oswald's teaching schedule allowed him the freedom to travel back to the east coast to speak on two occasions, and to spend a weekend in Columbus, Ohio, with the Quaker evangelist Charles Stalker. Author of the book *Twice Around the World with the Holy Ghost, or The Impressions and Convictions of the Mission Field*, Stalker had once stated, "People are going to the uttermost parts of the earth to take the beer that made Milwaukee famous—we must go and take the gospel that is the power of God unto salvation to them that believe."

68   Oswald Chambers: A Life in Pictures

Oswald Chambers with the Rev. Meredith Standley and his wife, Bessie, trustees of God's Bible School along with Minnie Ferle Knapp, widow of the school's founder. Martin Wells Knapp had started the college in the summer of 1900, as a training school for gospel workers, "where the Bible will be the main book studied" and "the Holy Ghost, its Author, will be acknowledged Superintendent and Interpreter." A Methodist minister and publisher of a periodical called *God's Revivalist*, Knapp chose the name "God's Bible School" to emphasize the institution's true ownership. When he died only a year later, at age forty-eight, his will stipulated that title for the school be placed in God's name; a local court later ruled that the Deity could not hold property in Hamilton County, Ohio. In a letter to his sister Florence, Oswald described Martin Wells Knapp as "a mighty man of God."

The Standleys's relationship with Oswald Chambers would continue over the next few years, as he returned to Cincinnati to speak at G.B.S. camp meetings in 1908, 1909, and 1910. Meredith and Bessie Standley would continue in God's Bible School leadership for more than four decades, until 1950.

While on a speaking trip to the east coast in February 1907, Oswald Chambers organized a winter retreat for the Standleys in Pennsylvania.

"Round the World All Right" 69

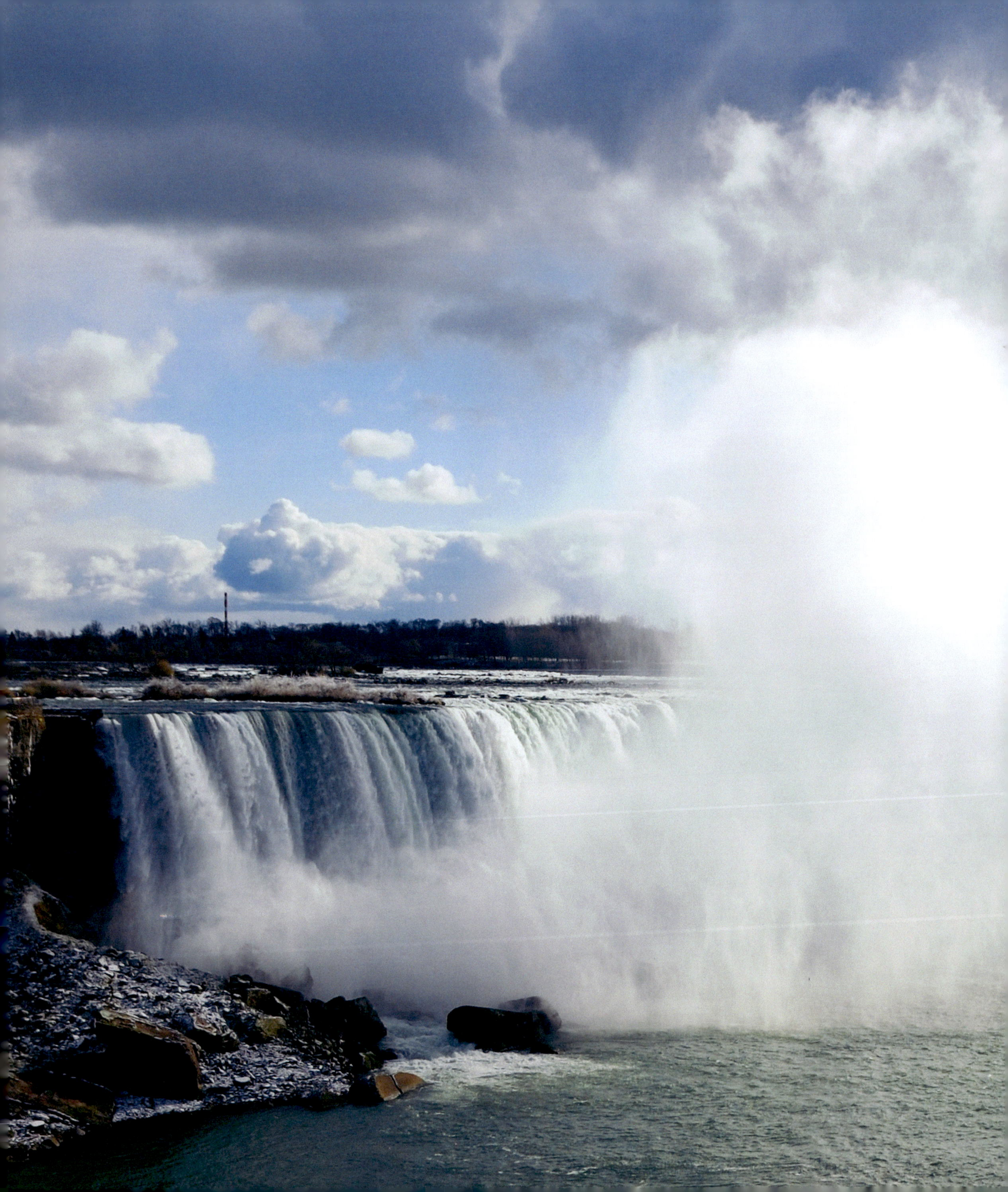

During that February 1907 tour, Oswald Chambers visited Niagara Falls, the international border between New York and Ontario, Canada. "Its dimensions are so enormous," he wrote to his youngest sister, Florence, "its fall of waters so colossal, the mountains of frozen mist, the icicles a hundred feet long—it is so great, so vast, and after hours of watching it gradually breaks into your conscious thinking that you are face to face with perhaps the most wonderful wonder in the natural world."

In his letters and diaries, Chambers often mentioned sunrises, sunsets, and other aspects of nature. En route to Seattle, where he would board a ship for Japan, Oswald commented on the "superb" scenery outside his railroad observation car: "The Rockies—I cannot hope to describe these to you. Massive unspeakable heights, all snow-clad, the air raw, piercing and cold; mighty pine trees are clustered in thousands all around; sublime rivers and waterfalls, and daring ingenious railways. It all needs to be seen to be realized ever so faintly."

Eight years later, during a class he taught at the Bible Training College in London, Chambers would say, "The matter of God's creation is a satisfaction to God, and when we come to know God by His Spirit, we are as delighted with His creation as He is Himself."

SCENES FROM HIS LIFE

When he reached Tokyo, Oswald Chambers met Charles and Lettie Cowman, former students of God's Bible School, who had arrived six years earlier to preach the gospel and begin a Japanese Bible school. Along with Juji Nakada and E. A. Kilbourne, they formed the Oriental Missionary Society, later known as OMS International and One Mission Society.

"I do not know what I expected," Chambers wrote in his diary, "but I never expected such an elaborate, splendidly organized work as it is. It was founded by Bros. Cowman and Kilbourne, and Nakada is their head evangelist and preacher. . . . He is really a deservedly great man among all here. Cowman and Kilbourne agree to this and certainly the students adore him. I am charmed with the premises, they exceed all I had dreamt of. Well-laid-out grounds and plenty of well-appointed houses. Mrs. Cowman is a royal soul and truly a saint."

Today, many know Lettie Cowman for *Streams in the Desert*, the devotional book she published in 1925.

72 Oswald Chambers: A Life in Pictures

Sunrise over the Red Sea, a sight that arrested Oswald Chambers's attention on his journey home from the United States and Japan. His diary and letters from early October 1907, while sailing through the Red Sea and the Gulf of Suez, contain exclamations such as, "A lovely morning," "A glorious and boisterous morning," and "What a sunrise!"

Chambers was especially stirred near the place where Moses received God's Law. "Imagine it, at 12 o'clock today, we were abeam of Mt. Sinai!" he wrote to his brother Arthur. "It is a lonely, fierce, paralyzing desert, full of the great ache of speechless loneliness and arid heat, brooding with unspoken and unfathomable mystery—nothing familiar, nothing usual, nothing homely; for thousands of centuries the scarred, serried range of sand-blighted mountains has held the mystery of God's purposes." Oswald was struck by the petty smallness of "modern civilization making its boast of progress," but was quickly reminded of Jesus Christ, a thought that came with "ineffable peace."

D. W. Lambert, author of the brief biography *Oswald Chambers: An Unbribed Soul* (1968), wrote, "Little did he know as he sailed past the coast of Egypt, that a few years later, that was to be his final scene of service."

"Round the World All Right"

An undated photo of League of Prayer leaders, including Oswald Chambers (standing, second from right) and James Gardiner (seated, second from left). Gardiner, a potato farmer by trade, had introduced Oswald to Juji Nakada, and the three together had visited northern Scotland to share the holiness message.

6 THE LEAGUE OF PRAYER

*What I owe to the League of Prayer
only our heavenly Father knows.*

OSWALD CHAMBERS, *letter of November 13, 1908*

Sixteen years after Oswald's death, Biddy Chambers published a book of reminiscences by family, friends, and scores of people his ministry had touched. One challenge of assembling the manuscript, she noted, was that several of those who wrote had known Oswald for many years, "hence the impossibility of keeping various contributions strictly to one period." Oswald's League of Prayer era, covering many years and overlapping other experiences, also defies easy classification.

Oswald was still at Dunoon when he first attended a League assembly; in that 1901 meeting, in the words of Mrs. Duncan MacGregor, "he was brought to claim a definite Baptism of the Holy Spirit." From 1911 to 1915, the League backed Oswald's Bible Training College venture in London.

Throughout the years between, Chambers would travel widely and speak tirelessly, often in support of the League's mission—to bring believers of various denominations together, asking God to fill them with the Holy Spirit, to revive churches, and to spread scriptural holiness. But amid his many obligations, he also found time to court and marry a young woman named Gertrude Hobbs.

The Pentecostal League of Prayer was the brainchild of a wealthy, prominent lawyer named Reader Harris, who founded it as an "interdenominational union of Christian people" in 1891. "What is needed today is a revival that will shake the Church," he wrote six years later. "I believe it can be brought about—and can only be brought about—by the *power of the Holy Ghost*, in answer to the believing prayer and faithful effort of individuals."

His message resonated with Oswald Chambers, who became an enthusiastic "missioner" throughout England, Scotland, Ireland, and Northern Ireland. "There were Conventions, and Bible readings with striking blackboard outlines, filled out and made clear by his own luminous expositions," one person recalled. "Many still bear witness to having found through these gatherings their 'Damascus road' where the Lord Himself appeared and apprehended them for life service."

One of those was the Rev. David Lambert, who later helped Biddy Chambers publish much of Oswald's teaching. He first encountered Chambers in 1908, at a League convention in the North Sea town of Sunderland. "I was arrested by the vigorous style and virile message of a young minister with a Scottish accent," Lambert recalled. "I knew nothing of his previous career, of the extraordinary leading of God he had known in his own life, but that afternoon there came through to my heart the authentic message of the Living God by the lips of His servant."

Richard Reader Harris (1847–1909) began his career in engineering, then studied law. Having accepted Christ through the influence of his wife, he added the ministry to his career—preaching, writing books, and establishing the Pentecostal League of Prayer.

Under the League's auspices, in autumn 1906, Chambers had spoken throughout England and Scotland with Juji Nakada. Then, after their ten-month tour of North America and Japan, Oswald quickly returned to League of Prayer business, leading a nine-day mission in November 1907 at the organization's Speke Hall headquarters in London. One woman reported that Chambers "spoke of the kind of suffering that glorifies God," and some people "revolted against its severity." But those with right hearts, she said, found "Jesus only, Jesus ever."

For the next six months, Chambers blanketed the island, from his hometown of Aberdeen, on Scotland's northeastern coast, all the way to Plymouth, far to England's southwest. Teaching two or three times a day wearied even the man who loved to quote the apostle Paul in 2 Corinthians 12:15, "I will very gladly spend and be spent for you." Typical of Chambers, though, he responded in prayer. "O Lord," he wrote in his journal, "this day I have to speak in Thy name three times, and I am un-moved and uninspired till now. If Thou canst convey Thy mind to me in my spiritual dullness, Oh, for Jesus Christ's sake, do it."

A breather would come in late May 1908, when Oswald traveled again to America. Camp meetings in Ohio, Massachusetts, and Maine awaited, but not before several relaxing days aboard the *Baltic*, the same ship on which he and Nakada had sailed. For this trip, he would lack the fellowship of his Japanese friend—but he would enjoy the company of Miss Hobbs.

Speke Hall, the League of Prayer center in London, where Chambers often led services. Portions of his messages here were included in the books *Our Brilliant Heritage* and *Workmen of God*.

The League of Prayer 77

Oswald and "Truda," as her family called her, had first met a couple of years earlier, around Christmas of 1905. He was leading a mission at London's Eltham Park Baptist Church, pastored by his brother Arthur, when he was introduced to Gertrude, her sister, and their widowed mother. Many months would go by before their paths again intersected, but their next meeting would seem to be ordained.

As it happened, Truda was also sailing aboard the *Baltic*. With plans to visit a friend and take a job in New York, she needed someone to watch over her journey—or so her mother thought. Mrs. Hobbs wrote to Oswald, asking if he would be that protective guide, a request that both "embarrassed and delighted" Gertrude, her daughter Kathleen recalled decades later. He was willing, and over their ten-day journey, the thirty-three-year-old evangelist discovered an intellectual and spiritual connection with the twenty-four-year-old stenographer. As he did for many friends and acquaintances, Oswald devised a nickname for Gertrude: Beloved Disciple. That would be abbreviated to B.D., which soon become Biddy, a name that would distinguish her from Oswald's sister Gertrude.

Once in America, Oswald and Biddy said farewell, and he continued on to Cincinnati for another camp meeting. But they began a correspondence that drew them even closer together. Only a few weeks after their passage, Oswald wrote from Cincinnati about the "sad and sordid sorrows of so many blighted lives," but noted that "it is a great refreshment to think of you." By August 19, he was writing, "All in His good time, we have the love, thank God."

Oswald and Gertrude, as man and wife, about ten years after their first meeting. They are dressed for a mission of the League of Prayer, an organization that touched on their entire married life.

78   Oswald Chambers: A Life in Pictures

The couple's letters would soon traverse the Atlantic, after Oswald returned to England for more League of Prayer work—including a "special mission" planned for Speke Hall from November 8–16. Biddy sailed home in time for this mission, which was indeed special—partway through it, during a visit to St. Paul's Cathedral, she and Oswald became engaged.

But there was little time for celebration, as Oswald began a ten-day mission in Belfast, Northern Ireland, just a week later. In the weeks to come, he would lead other missions in Portrush and Antrim, Northern Ireland, and Lowestoft, England, as well as conducting League business throughout Scotland and Yorkshire. Then, in late March 1909, came stunning news of the death of Reader Harris.

Felled by a stroke at age sixty-one, Harris was succeeded in League leadership by his wife, Mary—not Oswald Chambers. As he said in a eulogy of Reader Harris, "I would like to remind every Leaguer here that, although we have lost the clarion voice and personality of the leader sent forth by God, we have still got a leader amongst us in his wife, and may the Lord bless her!" While Mary Harris oversaw the organization's affairs from London, Oswald would repeat the cycle of his previous year—sail to the United States for a few months of camp meetings, then return to England for various League of Prayer events.

His final trip to America, from early June through late September 1910, featured stops in Ohio, Massachusetts, Maryland, Maine, and the Catskill Mountains of New York. It also included Biddy, traveling as Mrs. Oswald Chambers. They had been married on May 25.

The Pentecostal League of Prayer's newspaper, *Tongues of Fire*, with an advertisement at bottom promoting Oswald Chambers's November 8–16, 1908, mission at Speke Hall. The League was not affiliated with the tongues-speaking Pentecostal movement that had begun in California in 1906. In years to come, the League would drop the term "Pentecostal" to reduce confusion. It would also change the paper's name to *Spiritual Life*.

The League of Prayer 79

A League of Prayer leadership portrait from about 1911, including Oswald Chambers in the back row, Biddy Chambers at front left, and Mary Harris, Reader's widow, at center front. The man at far left is the Rev. David Lambert, who would later assist Biddy in "the work of the books"—publishing Oswald's teaching after his death.

The newlyweds returned to England in late September, and Oswald quickly launched into a heavy teaching schedule organized by John Skidmore, League of Prayer secretary in Manchester. Once, while hiking the English moors in a storm, he and Chambers had discussed the need of a better-thinking "man in the pew" who could then prompt "the man in the pulpit" to better preaching. So beginning in October, for three days a week in three different cities, Oswald taught his course in Biblical Psychology.

But even better things were coming. Oswald had dreamed of a full-fledged school where students would live and learn and be "personally influenced by godly men long in the work," as he had written at Dunoon. By early December 1910, the League of Prayer had rented a large residence that could house such a facility. The word went out: in January 1911, the Bible Training College would open for business, under the direction of Oswald and Biddy Chambers.

SCENES FROM HIS LIFE

Shown wearing the ceremonial wig of a barrister, Reader Harris was named a "King's Counsel" by the British monarchy. In April 1909, Oswald Chambers eulogized Harris, who had died of a stroke at age sixty-one, "as a King's Counsellor to me in the very highest sense. From the first moment I met him his counsel and prayers have been to me those of a commander and a leader. I thank God that He allowed me to know something of this man who reverenced God and feared not man, a man who in these disenchanted days stood with feet on earth and head in heaven, a viceroy to whom the King of kings had 'given the fires that kindle, and the strength that sways'; a man who stood erect, alive and alert, whose 'male and conquering voice' filled many a barren life, and quickened to rejoicing many a soul who had forgotten joy. He had a clarion voice spiritually, and every remembrance of him is a bracing call to let our Lord and Saviour satisfy His heart and fulfil His purpose in me. His memory is a new nerve to strenuous service, and I love my Lord more than ever for allowing me the privilege of living in the same day as such a leader of His flock." Chambers described Reader Harris and his wife, Mary, as "the Lord's choicest saints."

The League of Prayer

SCENES FROM HIS LIFE

An undated photo of John Skidmore and his wife, May. John's role with the Pentecostal League of Prayer in Manchester, England, brought Chambers to their home for a weekend in November 1907, when, after a noon meal, they had a twelve-hour conversation about Oswald's experience with entire sanctification. In the book *Oswald Chambers: His Life and Work*, John Skidmore shared Chambers's May 1906 testimony at Exeter Hall, London, in which he described his preceding spiritual crisis as "four years of hell on earth."

Chambers and Skidmore worked closely together and developed a lasting friendship. In Oswald's final year of life, 1917, he was pleased to receive a letter from John's wife detailing her own spiritual progress. "She writes that some things have become a wonderful revelation to her," he wrote in his diary on February 11, "'Mr. Chambers had talked about it in his own way ever since we knew him, but now I thank God it is mine.' I like this because it means she is gaining her own as the result of thinking and not of any propagandist teaching. The latter destroys the spontaneous moral originality of the Spirit of God in a saint. Views from propagandist teaching are borrowed plumes; teaching is meant to stir up thinking, not to store with goods from the outside."

82 Oswald Chambers: A Life in Pictures

Mary Riley, wearing the black bonnet typical of the League of Prayer's early years. She first encountered Oswald Chambers when he taught at Speke Hall, then enrolled in his Bible Training College. "It was a joy and an inspiration to be in his presence for there radiated from him in a very real way the joyousness and beauty of a life that was entirely at God's disposal," she wrote for the 1933 book *Oswald Chambers: His Life and Work*. "He always made you think of God."

When "the Great War" brought the B.T.C. to an end, Mary Riley followed the Chambers family to Egypt. There, she helped Biddy provide food, drink, and a touch of home to the troops as Oswald ministered to their spiritual concerns. "Of Mary Riley what can I say?" Oswald Chambers wrote in his diary just a month before his death. "To have been with her and known her during these months and the past years has been to see a Christian woman indeed and a joyous mixture of Mary and Martha. God bless and be blest for Mary Riley." After Oswald's death, Mary would stay in Egypt for two years, continuing her work with the "Beloved Disciple."

The League of Prayer 83

For his marriage proposal to Gertrude Hobbs, Oswald Chambers chose St. Paul's Cathedral in London. In the seventeenth century, architect Sir Christopher Wren designed St. Paul's dome to rise 365 feet into the air; in Chambers's day, it was the tallest building in the city.

7 BELOVED DISCIPLE

*It will be such a meagre home we will have, you and myself
going heart and soul into literary and itinerating work for Him.
It will be hard and glorious and arduous.*

OSWALD CHAMBERS, *letter to Biddy*

Feelings for Gertrude Hobbs had taken Oswald Chambers by surprise, leaving his poetic soul at a loss for words. "I want to tell you that I am in love," he wrote his parents on October 28, 1908, "and it is quite such a new experience that it opens up so many unknown things that I do not know quite how to put it."

Nearly three years had passed since Gertrude and Oswald had first been introduced. From the date of his letter, it had been exactly five months since the two had sailed aboard the *Baltic* for America—he to speak in the east and Midwest, she to pursue work in New York City. That they were on a particular ship at the same time was simply coincidence.

That is if you believe in coincidence, and Chambers did not. "The circumstances of a saint's life are ordained by God, and not by happy-go-lucky chance," he later taught. "He is bringing us into places and among people and under conditions in order that the intercession of the Holy Spirit in us may take a particular line." That "line" included Oswald's marriage to a woman who would support his ministry wholeheartedly—and, after his death, grow it exponentially.

First, though, God had to convince Oswald Chambers that he needed a wife. "I have been more usually absorbed in *Him* and work for Him than even you would suppose," he wrote to his parents, "that this 'thing' has been a trial foreign to me." Out of the trial came "a sense I never had before, a sense of my own loneliness."

But that feeling was certainly not desperation. Despite their nine-year age difference, Oswald and Gertrude were obviously suited for each other—they were both quick to laugh, loved and played music, enjoyed the company of children and animals . . . and, most importantly, shared a deep faith in Christ.

During their Atlantic passage, Oswald had nicknamed Gertrude, and since parting ways in New York in early June, he and "Biddy" had corresponded regularly. By September 16, he was clearly thinking of marriage, writing that God "has all the circumstances in His hand—in His hand my whole life and yours with me must be for Him and not for domestic bliss."

Soon, Oswald was seeking the approval of Biddy's mother, who a few months earlier had asked him to watch over her daughter on the *Baltic*. "Do you object to my corresponding with your youngest daughter, Gertrude?" he wrote. "I love her, and naturally would like to write her and see her occasionally as my missions allow. But we should like to know that this is with your sanction and certain knowledge of the kind of friendship forming."

Mrs. Hobbs, unclear on "the kind of friendship forming," asked Oswald to explain. He did, just a few days later: "I certainly do not mean 'Platonic' . . . but I do mean a friendship with view to an engagement and ultimate marriage."

Gertrude Hobbs with family and friends, around the time of her journey to New York. Oswald Chambers's future wife is seated at front left, holding a friend's hand. Her mother, Emily Amelia, is seated between Gertrude's brother, Herbert, and sister, Edith, called Daisy or "Dais" (far right).

One could never accuse Oswald of painting too rosy a picture of Biddy's prospects with him. "I have nothing to offer you but my love and steady lavish service for [God]," he wrote on October 23. "I can hear you say: Foxes have holes . . . but the Son of man hath not where to lay His head. I have His Word, let us both take it, subsequent days will prove His meaning in it—Let us go forth unto Him, without the camp, bearing His reproach." But Biddy was game, and three weeks later, when Oswald proposed marriage, she accepted.

Though Oswald was clearly the dominant personality, Biddy's quiet but tireless support was noticed and appreciated by many. Mary Hooker, daughter of the League of Prayer's Reader Harris, believed Oswald "had been equipped by God as a teacher, and his wife was to him the helpmeet he needed." Oswald certainly recognized the importance of a committed, capable wife. "I am finding out how much Mrs. Reader Harris was behind her husband," he wrote to Biddy as his fiancée. "The public saw him, but she was the power behind the throne. Blessed be the name of God. He is preparing us both for the same power and service."

That service required some sacrifices, and almost immediately. Within days of their engagement, Oswald left for nearly three months of League of Prayer business in Northern Ireland and Scotland. In the summer of 1909, he sailed alone for America, a trip of about ten weeks. But the next time he visited the United States, it would be with his wife at his side.

London's iconic Anglican cathedral, St. Paul's, viewed from the west. Oswald Chambers and Gertrude Hobbs were engaged here on November 13, 1908.

Beloved Disciple 87

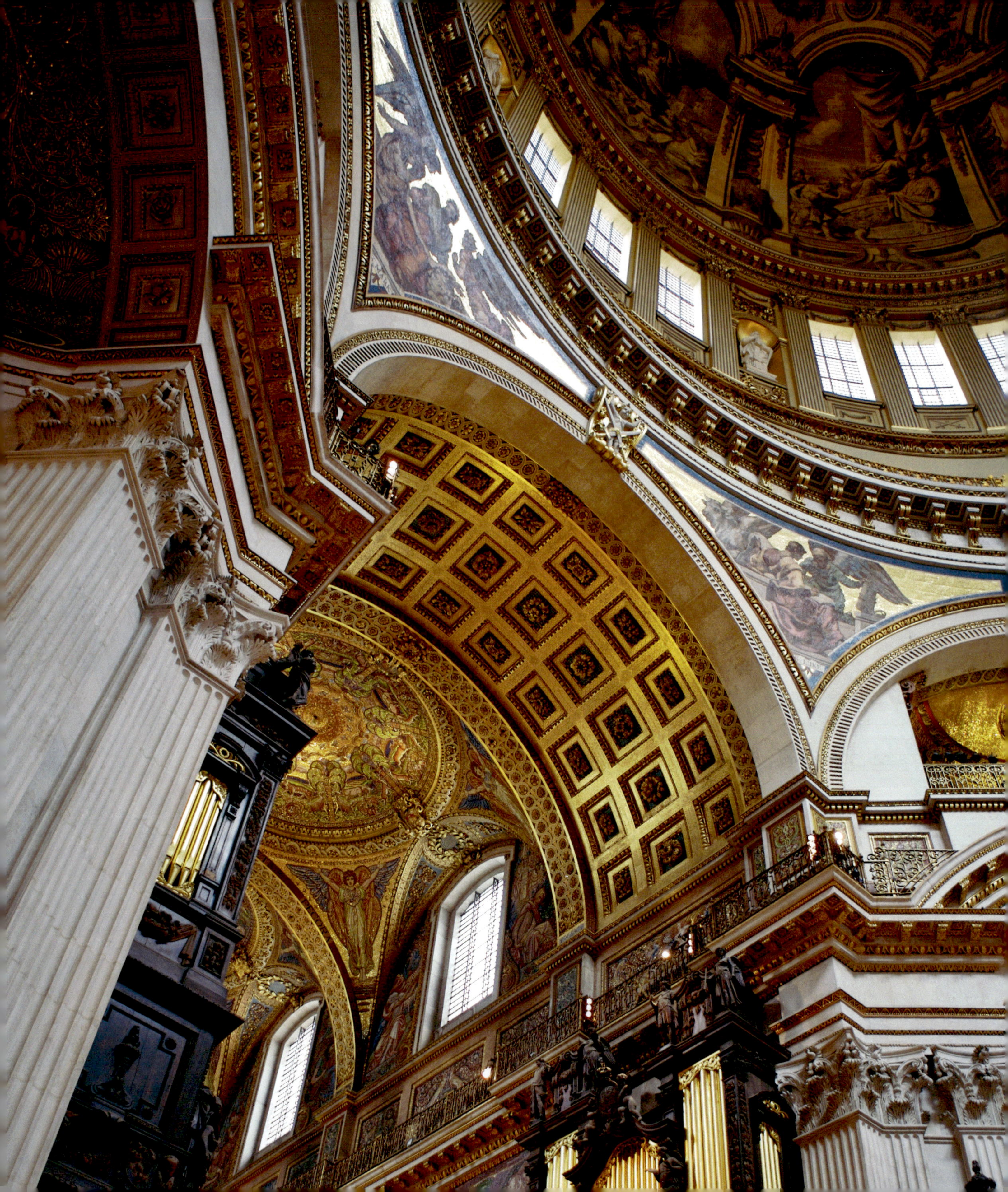

Mr. and Mrs. Oswald Chambers, with their wedding party—niece Doris (Arthur's daughter) in front, and from left to right at back, Oswald's friend Percy Lockhart, Biddy's sister Daisy, Oswald's sister Gertrude, and Biddy's brother Herbert. Lockhart, who Oswald had nicknamed "Summum Bonum" (the supreme good), was best man. The two had met when Chambers spoke at the Lockhart family's church in Dunstable, England.

OPPOSITE: Interior view of the dome of St. Paul's Cathedral.

Miss Hobbs became Mrs. Chambers on May 25, 1910, in a service conducted by Oswald's oldest brother. Though Arthur had led the Eltham Park Baptist Church, where the couple had first met, the wedding was held in a nearby chapel registered for such ceremonies. It seems appropriate that Oswald and Biddy were married in a Wesleyan Methodist church, since their honeymoon trip to the United States would include visits to several Holiness meetings.

They sailed from Liverpool aboard the *Caronia*, a Cunard Line ship, on May 31. After landing in New York City, Biddy stayed with a friend for much of June while Oswald, for the fourth straight year, went on to the God's Bible School camp meeting.

The newlyweds then reunited in Rossburg, Ohio, a hundred miles north of Cincinnati, where they spent two weeks in the "humble country home" of Hattie Hittle. She had met Oswald at the 1908 camp and, with her husband, hosted him on his return in 1909. This summer, the Hittles enjoyed both Oswald and Biddy's company.

"It was a very busy time on the farm," Hattie wrote years later, "but the holy communion and restfulness in the Holy Ghost was so gloriously manifested that the whole machinery ran evenly and its smoothness delighted our souls. My husband would slip in at noon hours and in sweet communion we would drink in the deep truths as given us by Brother Chambers, then with tear-dimmed eyes he would go out to his work."

For much of the next three months, meetings in Maryland, Massachusetts, and Maine occupied the couple's time. They did, however, schedule one week just to themselves in the Catskills of New York.

Beloved Disciple

But even then the couple was working, setting the stage for the ministry by which Oswald would gain worldwide fame: the published word. The year before their marriage, he had written to Biddy, "I want us to write and preach; if I could talk to you and you shorthand it down and then type it, what ground we could get over! I wonder if it kindles you as it does me!"

Now, surrounded by what Biddy called "the exceedingly grand and beautiful Catskill mountains," they put Oswald's dream to the test: he dictated an article based on Psalm 121:1–2. Called "The Place of Help," it would become the first chapter in a 1935 book of the same title, assembled from Oswald's Sunday sermons, Y.M.C.A. talks in Egypt, and Bible Training College lectures.

The college was, at this point, simply another dream of Oswald's fervent soul. But with Biddy ready and willing to support him in whatever came next, it too would soon become reality—in the seemingly haphazard ways in which Oswald Chambers often found God's ultimate order.

―――――◆―――――

This property in Elka Park, New York, advertised as a "fine family resort," served as a honeymoon retreat for Oswald and Biddy Chambers. Meadow Lawn allowed the couple to unwind briefly amid the busyness of Oswald's preaching and teaching tour of the states—but also take a first step toward "the work of the books."

SCENES FROM HIS LIFE

The newlyweds in Old Orchard, Maine, one stop on a four-month American honeymoon that doubled as a speaking tour for Oswald. To the left of Chambers is the Rev. Arthur Greene, a holiness preacher from Massachusetts; he was the companion of Oswald who, in Cincinnati in 1907, had shouted "I hate the devil!" on a city street (see page 62).

Beloved Disciple 91

SCENES FROM HIS LIFE

Two in a series of dated notes that Oswald Chambers gave Biddy to read each day on her journey to join him in Egypt, in December 1915. They include terms of endearment like "my darling Biddy" and "my beloved Biddy," which are not often found in other records of the couple's correspondence. "In view of Chambers's artistic, romantic nature, it may seem strange that his letters to Biddy did not contain more expressions of tenderness and love," wrote David McCasland in his definitive biography, *Oswald Chambers: Abandoned to God*. "In all likelihood they did, but only selected fragments of the originals survived. A man like Oswald Chambers, who wrote poetry, played classical music, and exulted in the beauty of nature, was not likely to restrict his written communications to spiritual and practical matters alone."

Some of Oswald and Biddy's correspondence was ultimately destroyed by their daughter, Kathleen. "There were some love letters," she told McCasland in a 1991 interview. "I had some but I threw them away. I didn't read them. I think that those kinds of letters were written between two people and not for anybody else. I hate the thought of other people reading letters that were as intimate as that. . . . They were very much in love with each other, that I do know."

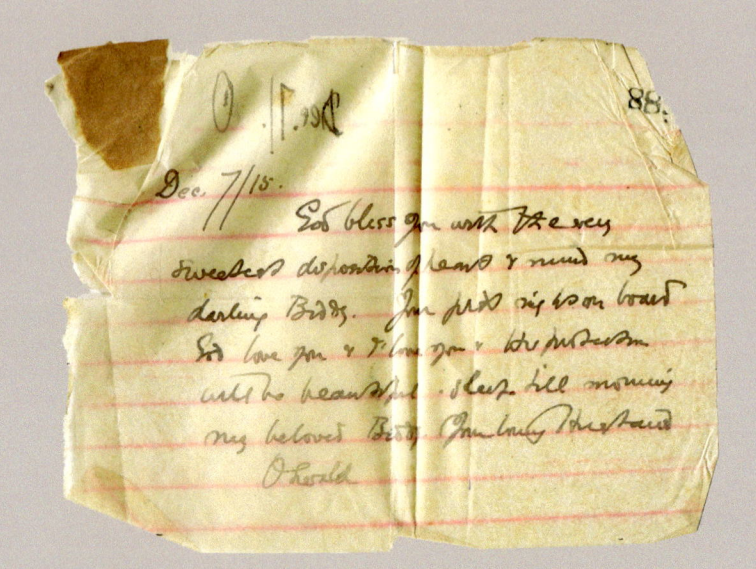

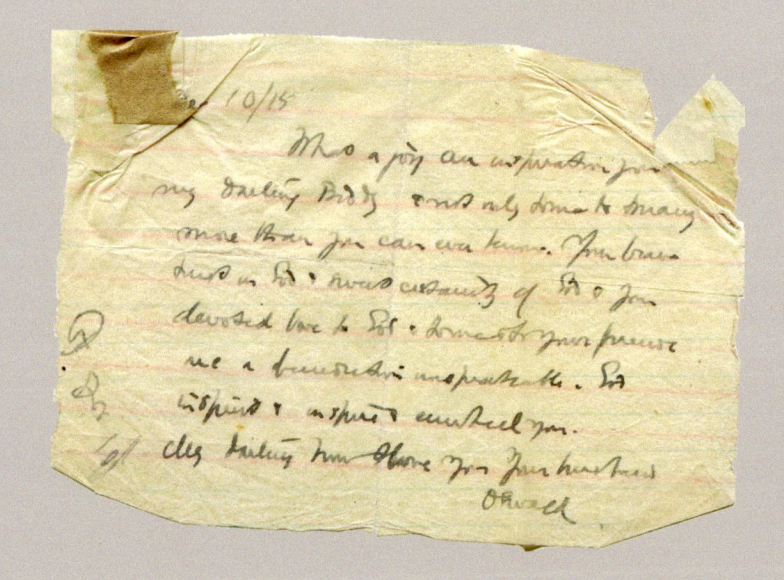

92 Oswald Chambers: A Life in Pictures

Married less than a week, Oswald and Biddy Chambers embarked on the *Caronia* at Liverpool, England, for their honeymoon journey to the United States. They traveled second class, with an assortment of shipmates listed on the passenger manifest by occupations such as miner, plumber, carpenter, civil engineer, mechanic, and school teacher. Beside many of the female passengers' names, as with Biddy's, was the notation "wife"; in the style of the day, two women were identified as "spinsters."

Oswald, who made the Atlantic passage four times and also sailed the Pacific from Seattle to Japan, enjoyed sea travel. On the Mediterranean, making his way to Egypt to serve with the Y.M.C.A., he noted in his diary, "They are beginning to call the life on board dull. My word! dull! with books and sea and mind and prayer, dull! It is teeming with endless and joyous interest. The vast expanse of sea is just great."

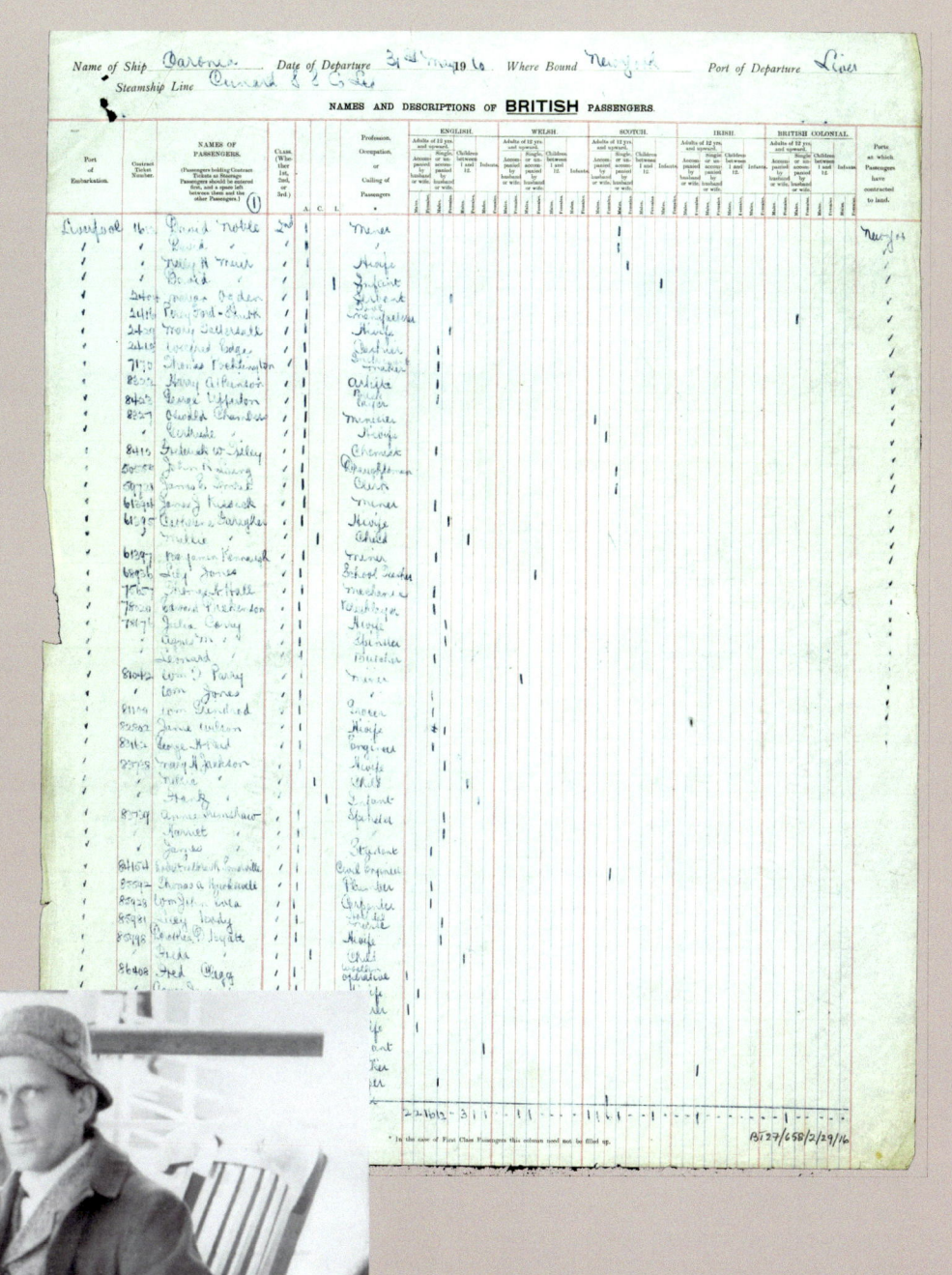

Oswald Chambers returning from the honeymoon trip aboard the *Adriatic*, September 1910.

Beloved Disciple 93

SCENES FROM HIS LIFE

"Amidst scenery which left us," Biddy Chambers recalled, "with the sense of worship expressed by Isaiah, 'The whole earth is full of His glory,'" the newlyweds collaborated on an article based on Psalm 121:1–2: "I will lift up mine eyes unto the hills, from whence cometh my help. My help cometh from the Lord, which made heaven and earth."

With her pad and pencil, she captured Oswald's thoughts:

> *Mountains stir intense hope and awaken vigour, but ultimately they leave the climber exhausted and spent. Great men and great saints stir in us great aspirations and a great hopefulness, but leave us ultimately exhausted with a feeling of hopelessness; the inference we draw is that these people were built like that, and all that is left for us to do is to admire. . . .*
>
> *To whom are you looking? To some great mountain-like character? Are you even looking at the Lord Jesus Christ as a great mountain-like character? It is the wrong way; help does not come that way. Look to the Lord alone, and come with the old pauper cry—*
>
> *Just as I am, without one plea*
> *But that Thy blood was shed*
>   *for me,*

94 Oswald Chambers: A Life in Pictures

*And that Thou bid'st me come to Thee—
O Lamb of God, I come.*

Any soul, no matter what his experience, that gets beyond this attitude is in danger of falling from grace. Oh, the security, the ineffable rest of knowing that the God Who made the mountains can come to our help!

The entire article, of approximately eighteen hundred words, became the first of Oswald's messages distributed to British soldiers after his death in November 1917. As Percy Lockhart, best man in the Chambers's wedding recalled, "A leaflet was printed and scattered among the men in Egypt and Palestine in time for Christmas. There was little thought at the time of the number of books to which this leaflet, entitled 'The Place of Help,' was to be the forerunner. . . . I have had the joy and privilege of being associated with the publishing from those early days right on until now; and with the growing demand for all the books, and for their translation into a number of languages, one feels confident that God will unfold yet more of His purpose in this great work."

LEFT: Catskill Mountains

Beloved Disciple

Clapham Common, the park area of southwest London abutting the Bible Training College building at 45 North Side. The structure in the center of the photo is a bandstand, built in 1890—two decades before Oswald Chambers started the school.

8 BIBLE TRAINING COLLEGE

To many the period of their training at the B.T.C.,
Bible Training College, will always remain as the greatest,
happiest and most gracious days of their life.

LILY BLIGHT, ADELAIDE, AUSTRALIA, *Oswald Chambers: His Life and Work*

For years, Oswald Chambers had dreamed of starting his own Bible college on the lines of those in Dunoon or Cincinnati. When God finally said "go," the teacher had a month to develop a school from scratch.

Only weeks after Oswald and Biddy arrived home from their honeymoon in America, League of Prayer leaders found a seemingly perfect building in London. Five stories tall, it featured a large reception area suitable for a lecture hall, plus enough rooms for some two dozen residential students and the newlywed administrators—he was the principal, she the "Lady Superintendent." The building was conveniently located, close to Mrs. Reader Harris's home, about a mile from Speke Hall, only steps away from public transportation.

The League rented the building in December 1910, announcing that the "Bible Training College" would open in January 1911. Without furnishings, curriculum, or students (and their tuition fees), the school would become a public example of Oswald Chambers's trust in the unseen, often unexpected, ways of God.

"God's order comes to us in the haphazard," Chambers later taught, words now part of the book *He Shall Glorify Me*. "We try to plan our ways and work things out for ourselves, but they go wrong because there are more facts than we know; whereas if we just go on with the days as they come, we find that God's order comes to us in that apparently haphazard way."

Haphazard, perhaps, but not meager—45 North Side was "an ideal house in an ideal position," according to Mary Hooker, Reader Harris's daughter and secretary of the school. "The large double drawing-room seemed almost too magnificent for a lecture hall," she recalled, with paneling, gilt mirrors, and an Italian scene painted on the ceiling. "It was wildly over-decorated," Katherine Ashe believed. But the surroundings prevented any sense of "bareness" from the simple furnishings: a blackboard for Oswald and chairs for the students.

Those chairs, in addition to furniture for the students' rooms, were funded by League supporters, who "responded wonderfully" to an appeal to outfit the new Bible Training College. With the physical plant ready, the B.T.C. could begin enrolling students—but that process might have tried the faith of anyone other than Oswald or Biddy Chambers.

Mrs. Hooker remembered the first applicant, a man who impressed Oswald in an interview and "was prepared to start at once, even before the Principal and his wife were in residence." Chambers himself showed the man to his room one evening, but he changed his mind during the night and disappeared. The young man at least had the courtesy to leave a note in the school's mailbox.

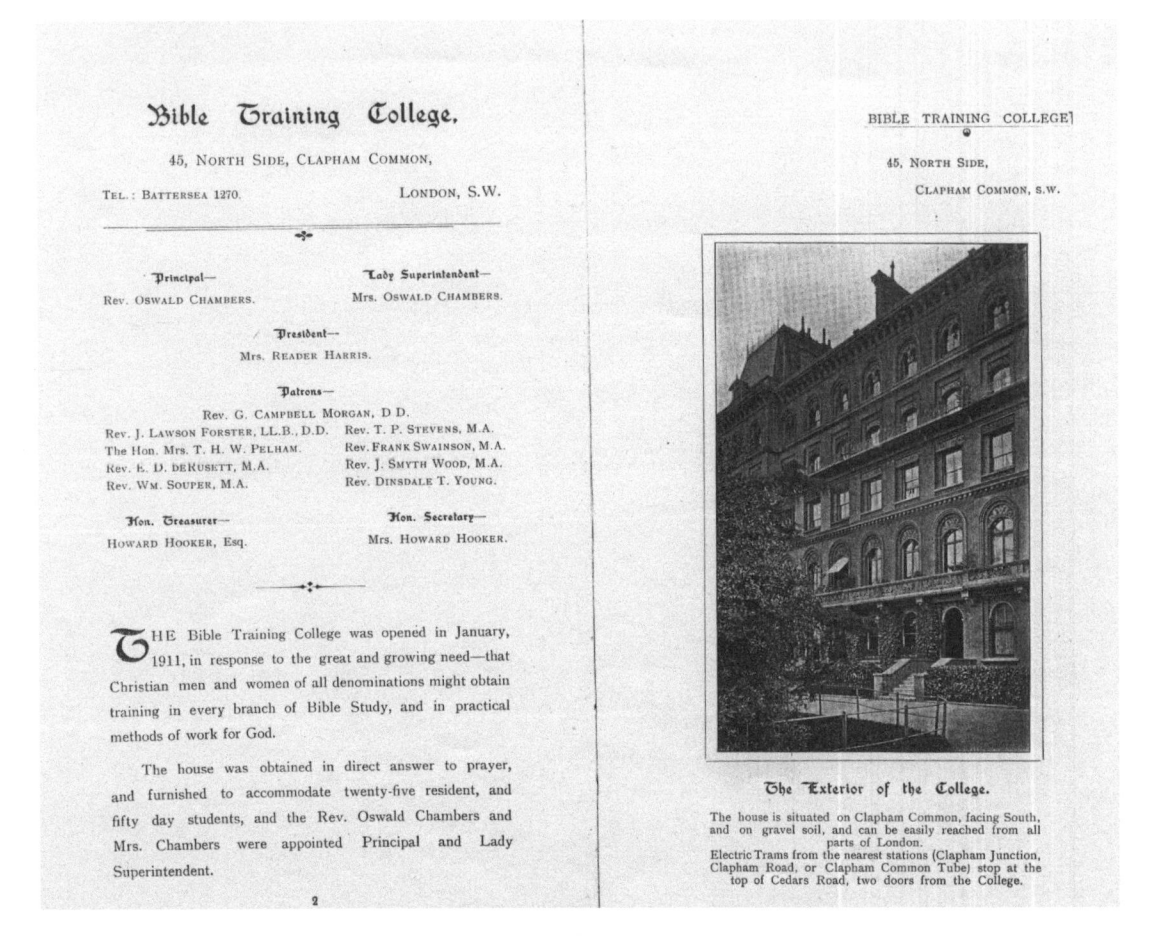

Two pages from an undated prospectus of the Bible Training College, showing the handsome building that faced the Clapham Common, "obtained in direct answer to prayer." The prayers did not stop with the acquisition of the building, according to *The Book of the College* by Katherine Ashe: "Before one soul entered that house, the Principal and his wife together visited every room, from attic to basement, and prayed that *there* the presence of the Spirit of God would create and maintain the atmosphere of His own abiding."

Katherine Ashe, converted under Oswald's preaching and later a student at the college, reported that in the B.T.C.'s first term, "there was one resident student only in all the big house." As D. W. Lambert described those days in *Oswald Chambers: An Unbribed Soul*, "Along with the Principal and Lady Superintendent, this student had meals at a little square table set like an oasis in the desert of the big dining room. Later she was to testify of the amazing blessing of those days that might have been so embarrassing."

In time, that student—who would become a missionary in the Belgian Congo—was joined by others, enough to fill the bedrooms. Men and women both, around a dozen each, came to live at 45 North Side, while up to fifty day students also enjoyed Oswald's leadership.

"The students!" Katherine Ashe recalled. "Such a mixed-up crowd of men and women! of all ages, all classes, all Protestant creeds. . . . There were a butler and a barrister, a clergyman's daughter and a mill-hand, a private in His Majesty's Army and a captain, a medical man and a cook, a writer of books and a fireman from his engine, all living in the house together . . . the difference in rank and skill, or in education, never having loomed large in the mind of any."

In the B.T.C.'s four years of existence (1911–15), there were 106 resident students and some three thousand others who walked in for classes. Several would highlight the impact of Chambers's prayer (he called it "the ministry of the interior"); others remembered his spiritual sensitivity, his uncanny ability to recognize and address unspoken needs—physical, financial, or otherwise. One wrote, "You felt as if he could read you through and through."

NOTICE.

"*All service ranks the same with God.*"

You are requested to kindly do your part in keeping this room tidy.

If you do not, someone else will have to.

In his teaching, Oswald Chambers was careful to point out that the Christian life is not one of "rules and regulations." As principal of the Bible Training College, he printed this single expectation on a card given to each residential student.

Bible Training College 99

Informal interaction with Oswald Chambers, the daily observation and absorption of his example, was a key to the school's mission. But the B.T.C.'s formal coursework was also vital. "Chambers was both a prophet and an evangelist, but he also had the gift of the teacher," Lambert wrote. "He loved to teach (and that is usually the mark of a good teacher)."

From his earliest days in the faith, as a sixteen-year-old in Peckham, Chambers had expounded the Bible. At Dunoon, he quickly progressed from student to teacher, becoming tutor of philosophy. Since spring 1909, he had lectured in various cities on topics such as "Christianity vs. Socialism" and "Biblical Psychology"; within that period, he also oversaw a League of Prayer correspondence course in both Britain and the United States. To the modern observer, Oswald's workload is stunning—he personally read thousands of papers from hundreds of students, giving an individual response to each. These courses and lectures, his friend John Skidmore said, "proved the stream which eventually developed into the river of the Bible Training College."

The first B.T.C. courses were Biblical Psychology and Biblical Ethics, but as the student body grew, others were added, from New Testament Greek to Elocution. Student Howgate Greenwood, later a minister in South Africa, had previously known Chambers through his writings, his Manchester lectures, and his correspondence course. "He was a born teacher, forceful in his delivery, clear and convincing in his subject matter, accompanied by a deep and practical religious experience," Greenwood wrote. "His spiritual strength never dismayed one, rather it encouraged one to follow after him as he sought to follow his Master."

The newsletter of God's Bible School in Cincinnati, announcing "Bro. Oswald Chambers' Bible School Correspondence Classes," an American version of courses the League of Prayer offered in Britain. By 1915, when he felt God's call to the war effort in Egypt, Chambers served more than nineteen hundred enrollees. Essays might receive a response like, "Your implications are very fine and penetrating, and I think your explicit statements along with the implied ones make a thoroughly satisfactory exegesis."

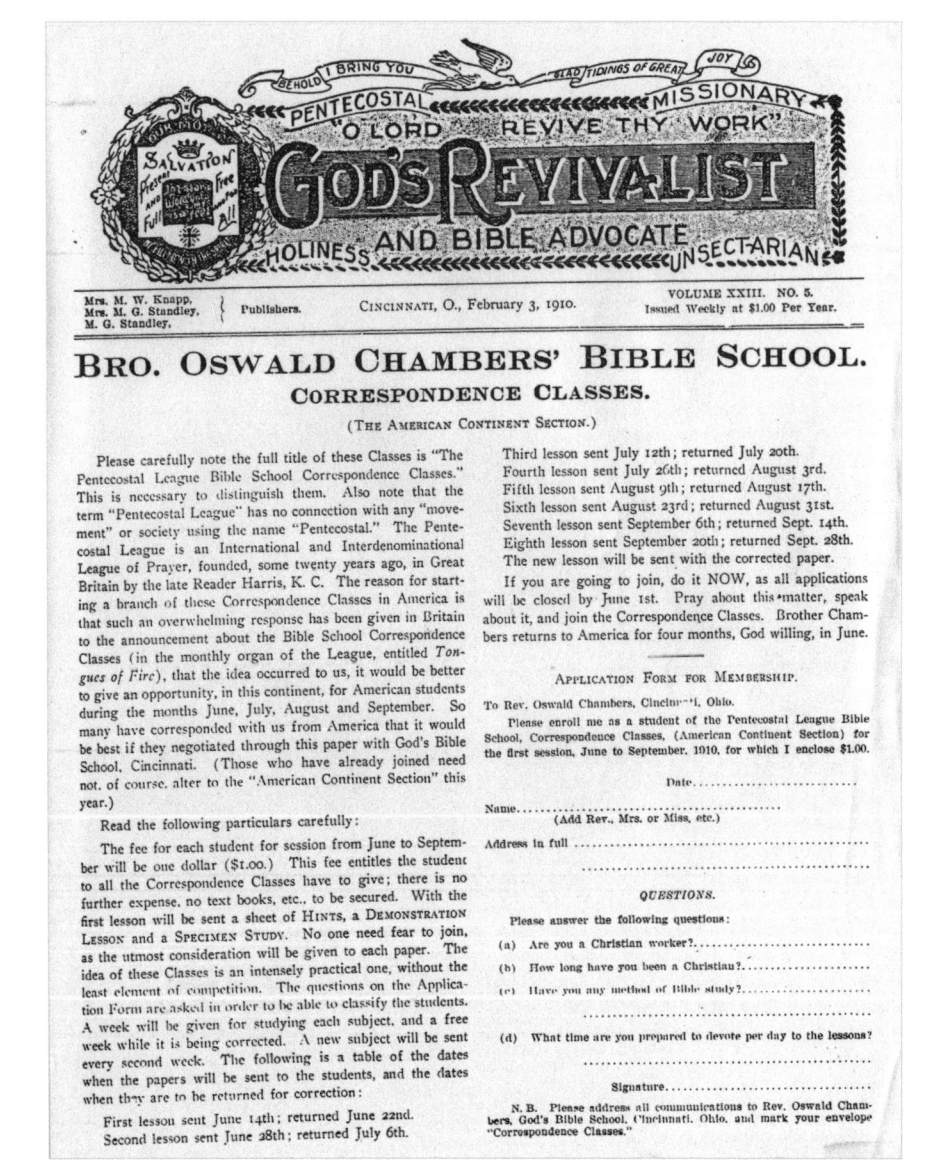

Though Oswald Chambers was the acknowledged leader of the school, "the man sent from God," as a B.T.C. brochure put it, he had plenty of help. Biddy, as "Lady Superintendent," would take shorthand notes of all his lessons and teach a class in Bible memorization. Mrs. Hooker, the school secretary, led a Bible survey class. Katherine Ashe, well into her forties when she became a student, went on to teach Christian Sociology.

Local ministers were called upon to lead courses on Sunday school programs. The renowned pastor, author, and Bible scholar G. Campbell Morgan spoke for the school's first anniversary. And a missions class in 1915 featured C. T. Studd, once England's most famous cricket player, a wealthy man who gave away his inheritance to serve God in China, India, and Africa.

But perhaps the most compelling personality of all at the Bible Training College was the one who arrived on May 24, 1913—Oswald and Biddy's only child, Kathleen.

The Bible Training College family—students, staff, and "little Kathleen"—in 1914. The Chambers family is seated in the second row; to the right of Oswald is Mrs. Reader Harris, while to her right are her son-in-law and daughter, Mr. and Mrs. Howard Hooker, the school's treasurer and secretary, respectively. To Mrs. Hooker's right is Katherine Ashe, who joined the B.T.C. as a student before taking on teaching duties herself.

A self-described agnostic, Ashe met Chambers when he preached in Belfast and stayed in the boardinghouse where she lived. "I recall the groan of dismay when we learned a 'Missioner' was to be a guest in the house, for we had recently suffered many things in spirit on account of a man who made preaching his trade," she wrote after Oswald's death in Egypt. "Tacitly, we ignored the newcomer for some days until his innate charm of manner and unmistakable reality in speech and manner first shamed us, and then altogether won us to welcome him into our circle." When she attended one of Chambers's meetings, she found herself yielding to Christ's claims, "a wholly supernatural 'conversion' in a meeting to which a purely conventional courtesy had led me."

Bible Training College

One day before their third anniversary, Oswald and Biddy Chambers experienced firsthand the pain and the joy of childbirth. The delivery was difficult, but the baby thrilled her parents—and the entire Bible Training College family. "Through those years there ran," Katherine Ashe recalled, "the golden thread of Kathleen's life and being."

Oswald had a natural affinity for children, perhaps because he saw in them a glimpse of the Christian life as it should be: "The life of a child is unconscious in its fullness of life, and the source of its life is implicit love." Years after his death, mature adults wrote of his close attention to, and natural interaction with, their younger selves. "A visit from him was always an event," his niece Irene said. "He reveled in the pranks of my small brothers and egged them on to all sorts of absurdities."

Now, two months shy of his thirty-ninth birthday, Chambers was overjoyed to have a child of his own. "Give my love to my precious little baby," he wrote Biddy from Scotland the next year. "I can scarcely bear to ask of her, she is so precious to my mind."

But he also sensed a danger, even in "God's gift to us": when Kathleen was three months old and undoubtedly the belle of the B.T.C., Oswald wrote to Biddy, "Do not allow the influence of the many loving women around you to turn your heart away from God's supreme call of us both with Kathleen to His service." By Kathleen's second birthday, Oswald had come to believe that that service would be to soldiers of the British Empire.

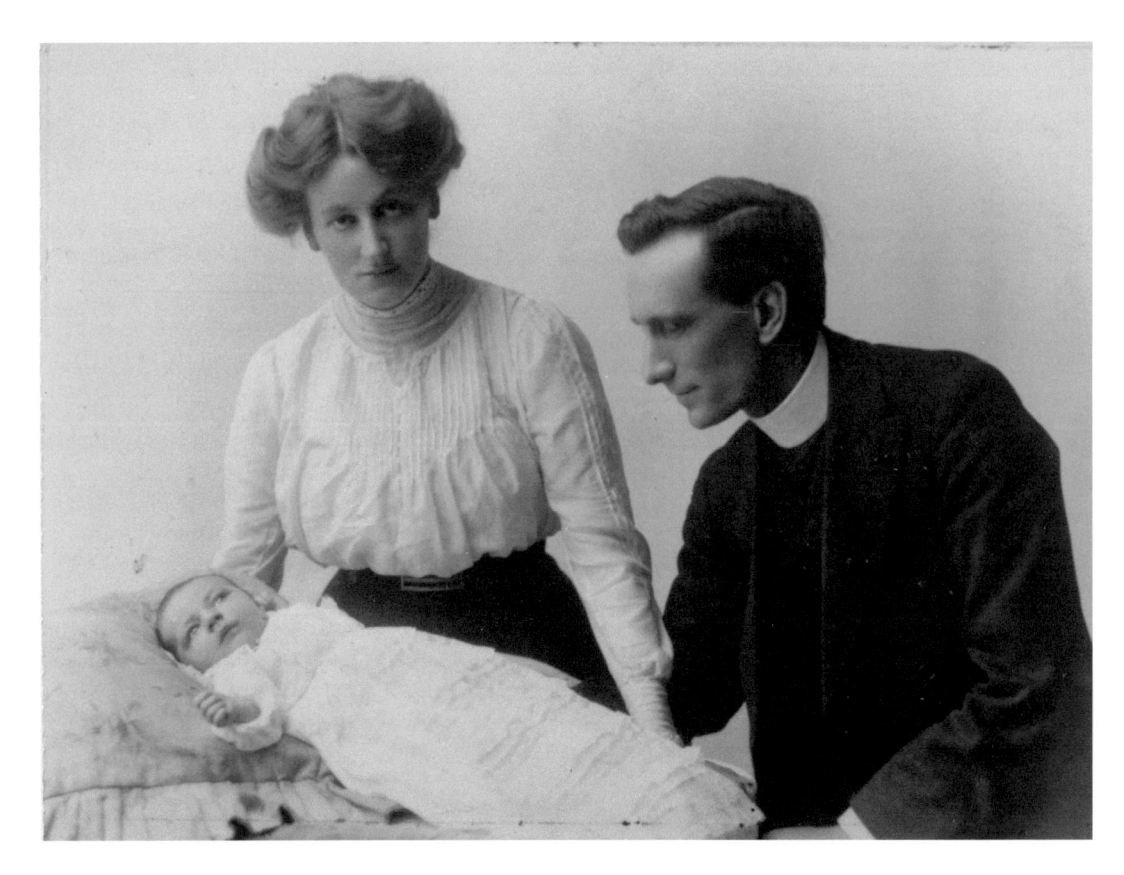

Kathleen Marian Chambers was born on May 24, 1913. Exactly three years later, in Ismailia, Egypt, Oswald wrote in his diary, "To-day is not only Empire Day, but Kathleen's birthday. God be praised for our little daughter, and cause her to be a sister of the Lord Jesus Christ."

102 Oswald Chambers: A Life in Pictures

Though it wasn't immediately obvious, the "Great War" that engulfed Europe in the late summer of 1914 signaled the beginning of the end for the Bible Training College. Its autumn session began September 26, just four days after a single German submarine, to that point a weapon of unrecognized effectiveness, sank three British battleships in the North Sea. In about an hour, some fourteen hundred men were lost.

Oswald Chambers recognized the fear such circumstances created. "We are scared and terrorized when our social order is broken, when thousands of men are killed, and well we may be," he would say in 1916. "But how many of us in times of peace and civilization bother one iota about the state of men's hearts towards God? Yet that is the thing that produces pain in the heart of God, not the wars and devastations that so upset us."

The spiritual needs of the fighting men weighed on Chambers's heart, and staying at the B.T.C. created a pressure "all but unendurable." Still, Chambers wrote to his parents, "I know God well enough not to confound my own natural desires and impulses for His will or ordering."

By late May 1915, he had decided to volunteer himself as a military chaplain, "'first aid' spiritually," as he described it. "Nothing is arranged or even clear by any means yet, nothing but my decision before the Lord," he told Hannah and Clarence in a letter. "I shall do my human best naturally, but as in many times in the past, I shall find God opening up the way. My mind is clear regarding God's call, the rest will 'fall out' or 'in' as He ordains."

The Chambers family in the Bible Training College garden in 1915, the year Oswald decided to serve British soldiers at war.

This placard for the *Times* of London advertises the paper of August 5, 1914, announcing England's entry into what we know as World War I. The assassination of Austrian Archduke Franz Ferdinand in late June led to Austria-Hungary's July 28 declaration of war on Serbia; within days, German aggression on the continent spurred England to join the fight. The Ottoman Empire (modern-day Turkey), allying with Austria-Hungary and Germany, expanded the war to the Middle East and set the stage for the final act of Oswald Chambers's life.

Bible Training College

Chambers sensed that he would serve with the Young Men's Christian Association, which provided physical and spiritual support to the troops—and soon, the organization did accept him for work in Egypt. After four years at the Bible Training College, he would wind down its work and transition his energies toward the Y.M.C.A.'s support of the British war effort. Biddy, he noted, was "just keen on the thing," and several from the B.T.C. would follow Oswald to the Egyptian desert.

In July 1915, at the end of its regular term, the college shut down—at least for the duration of the war. As was typical of Chambers, he left the question of its future open, to allow God to lead. In October 1917, shortly before his death, Oswald wrote to his former students, saying, "We send a message of good cheer, and a hearty reminder that the 'B.T.C.' still stands as our watchword, viz., 'Better to Come.' . . . In the immediate days after the war we may meet together again, or we may not; we may have another passing organization of the B.T.C., or we may not; but whatever transpires, it is ever 'The best is yet to be.'"

Before he embarked for the Middle East, though, Oswald took a well-deserved vacation to Yorkshire, some 250 miles northwest of London. Chambers loved to fish and hike in "the leagues of pure air" he found there, but this would not be a solitary journey—Biddy and Kathleen joined him, of course, along with other family members and friends from the college. When the holiday was over, he promptly began serving the soldiers training around nearby Wensleydale.

Oswald and Biddy Chambers, standing at center, in the Yorkshire village of Askrigg in August 1915. The group vacation, held between the closing of the Bible Training College and Oswald's work with the Y.M.C.A. in Egypt, also included Oswald's siblings Arthur (standing at left), Gertrude (middle row at left), and Bertha (middle row, center, holding Kathleen).

From Askrigg, on September 25, 1915, Oswald wrote to his mother, telling her that he would sail for Egypt in two weeks. The journey was just the next step in his ongoing pursuit of God:

When the word came—"Go ye into all the world," I went, and truly He made "all my ways" for they seemed certainly not mine or common sense. I had thought to settle in Dunoon College, in Japan, in America, and in the B.T.C., but His way for me is "the world."

In his prayer journal, Oswald Chambers had praised God for his time at the Bible Training College, calling it "four years of unique loveliness." Now, he was ready to give it up and leave it all behind, "because I believe I do so in answer to Thy call."

SCENES FROM HIS LIFE

Flo Gudgin, whom Oswald Chambers called "Gudgie," spent about two years at the Bible Training College before marrying Oswald's friend and coworker Jimmy Hanson. "What that time meant I cannot put into words," she wrote for the book *Oswald Chambers: His Life and Work*. "I know that, as I considered it, I was constrained to say before God—What have I done to be given so great a privilege? One of the outstanding impressions of those days was the terrifically high standard put before us, nothing less than our all and our utmost would suffice. Many a time we should certainly have said—'it is high, I cannot attain unto it,' but such words died on our lips for we saw in the Principal a walking edition of the truth he proclaimed, and the inspiration of his life made every spoken word quick and living. Those truths have become part of our very selves, and as labourers in His Kingdom have helped more than we can say. Mr. Chambers taught us many mighty truths, but chiefest of all was the fact that he centred us always in God Himself."

The Bible Training College building, 45 North Side, Clapham Common

Katherine Ashe, pictured here on the Yorkshire Moors, chronicled the B.T.C. experience in *The Book of the College*, and contributed reminiscences to the 1933 book *Oswald Chambers: His Life and Work*. For the latter, she wrote of the Bible Training College,

> *Two things of that time stand out in my mind especially. The first is the amazing way in which God poured the Truth, and deep interpretations of the Truth through [Oswald Chambers's] personality; and in doing so, richly blessed him with glimpses and apprehensions of further truths continually, so that we, listening and learning, gained a confident certainty of the inherently inexhaustible nature of Truth, and also the certainty that the Spirit of God does supernaturally use a man's mentality, his imagination, his intuitions, when the man himself is truly yielded to God.*
>
> *The other is, again, the wonderful gentleness and tenderness in so young a man, that made him able to deal with such varied men and women in the crises of their lives without wounding the spirit, and without deviating by a hair's breadth from the sternness of the standard set by his Lord.*

"Miss Ashe" also noted "the enormous amount of work, accomplished with such slender physical resources." A printed prospectus for the college encouraged friends to contribute toward its financial needs. "The College is not self-supporting," the brochure read. "It has been maintained day by day in direct answer to prayer, through the help of the Lord's 'stewards.' The fees do not nearly cover the actual expenses."

BIBLE TRAINING COLLEGE.
45, NORTH SIDE,
CLAPHAM COMMON, S.W.

The Lecture Hall.

The Lecture Hall can accommodate from 70 to 80 people. It is seated with Institute chairs, having an arm on the right side, which forms a small table on which to take notes. These chairs cost 7/6 each, and many of them have been "adopted" by friends, who provide the cost. The chair is then marked on the back with a label, giving their name. Several of the "adopted" chairs are seen in the picture. Notice also the painted ceiling, pillars, and gilt mirrors left by the owner for College use, and the blackboard prepared for a lecture by the Principal.

Bible Training College

SCENES FROM HIS LIFE

The Autumn 1914 syllabus of the Bible Training College provides synopses of courses taught mainly by Oswald Chambers, with assistance from Biddy Chambers, Katherine Ashe, and others. Gladys Ingram, shown here later in life with her daughter, Audrey, and husband, Vyvyan Henry Donnithorne, recalled Oswald Chambers's personal example as a powerful addition to the coursework. "By living Christ daily before us at the B.T.C., he showed me the difference between religion and Reality," she wrote for *Oswald Chambers: His Life and Work*. "I had been brought up in a Christian home, and as I grew up took some part in Church work, and really came to the B.T.C. to get preparation for missionary service abroad, and there through coming in contact with the Principal, I realized that I knew *about* the Lord Jesus Christ, but did not know *Him*." The woman nicknamed "Gladiolus" by Oswald Chambers said she came to understand the truth of 2 Corinthians 5:17—"If any man be in Christ, he is a new creature: old things are passed away; behold, all things are become new."

108   Oswald Chambers: A Life in Pictures

Philip and Gertrude Hancock both studied under Oswald Chambers at the Bible Training College, then ministered with him in Egypt. When they wrote reminiscences for *Oswald Chambers: His Life and Work*, they were married and serving God in western Persia (Iran).

"The B.T.C. meant to me, first, fellowship with a man of God who brought me face to face with Christ as Lord," Philip wrote. "There was no pretence, no mere religiosity, but just rugged reality. Mr. Chambers' life was always a great challenge. We realized this in the College days and we still feel it in our innermost spirit. Yet it was never to himself he drew us, but to the One Who was his very life and his beloved Master."

Hancock also recalled "the blessing of associations with the B.T.C. family (one of whom became my wife) in London and also in Egypt, and there is ever that bond in the spirit between us all which is a very precious reality."

Gertrude earned *two* nicknames: "Woodbine" and "Bill." She wrote, "It is a joy to look back to the days when I first became acquainted with Mr. Chambers in the B.T.C. After a few weeks there of real spiritual refreshing, God spoke to me through a message of Mr. Chambers', and I recognized unmistakably that it was God's call to step out in faith in Him and prepare for Christian service. . . . I had the rare privilege of being in Egypt with Mr. Chambers and working under his leadership and inspiration; and the call still comes to grow in the knowledge of Him and help others to know Him too."

Bible Training College

SCENES FROM HIS LIFE

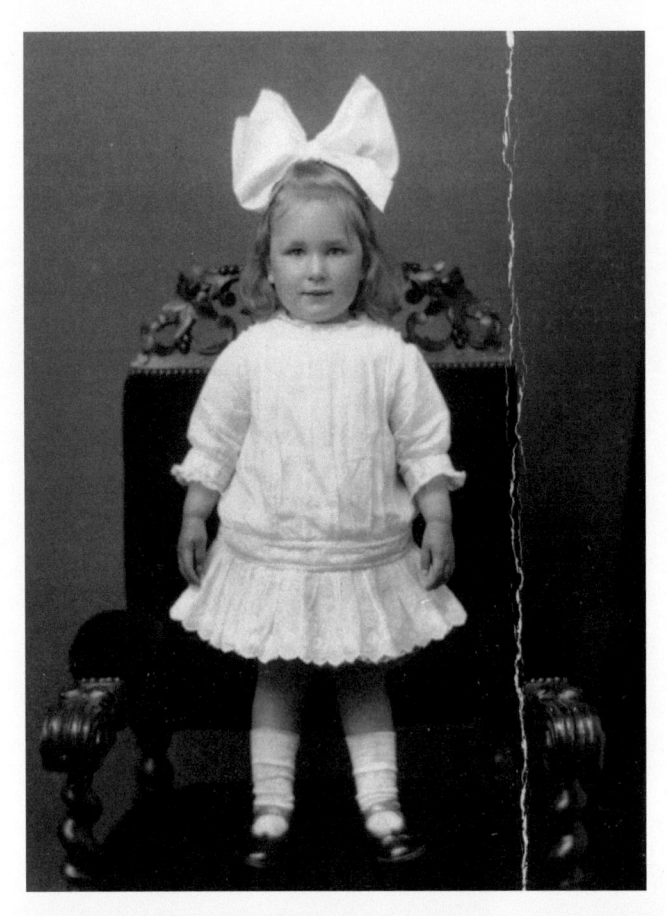

A series of portraits from 1915, highlighting two-year-old Kathleen Chambers. The poem of a Scottish soldier in Egypt likely speaks both for his fellow military men and the students of the Bible Training College:

There's little Kathleen, winsome sprite,
Sae full of a' that's pure and bright,
A glimpse that gladdens aye the sight
A child-life growing.
In her was life and love and light
And joy o'erflowing.

"It was strange and wonderful to see her touch upon us all," Katherine Ashe wrote in *The Book of the College*. "Old and young, commonplace and odd, dull or brilliant, cultured or ignorant, there was not one of us whose life was not touched by those baby fingers. . . . She was a very human, bonnie, darling Baby, and she became a centre round which the love of all the grown-up men and women could be poured."

110 Oswald Chambers: A Life in Pictures

Candid photos of the beloved "little Kathleen" at the Bible Training College. In his study of the life of Job, *Baffled to Fight Better*, Oswald Chambers contrasted Zophar, the self-styled "moral superior" of Job, with a child in its innocence. "God uses children, and books, and flowers in the spiritual instruction of a man, but he seldom uses the self-conscious prig who consciously instructs. . . . There are no experts in spiritual matters as there are in scientific matters. The spiritual expert is never so consciously because the very nature of spiritual instruction is that it is unconscious of itself; it is the life of a child, manifesting obedience, not ostentation. Our Lord describes the spiritual expert in Matthew 18:4—'Whosoever therefore shall humble himself as this little child, the same is greatest in the kingdom of heaven.'"

Bible Training College   111

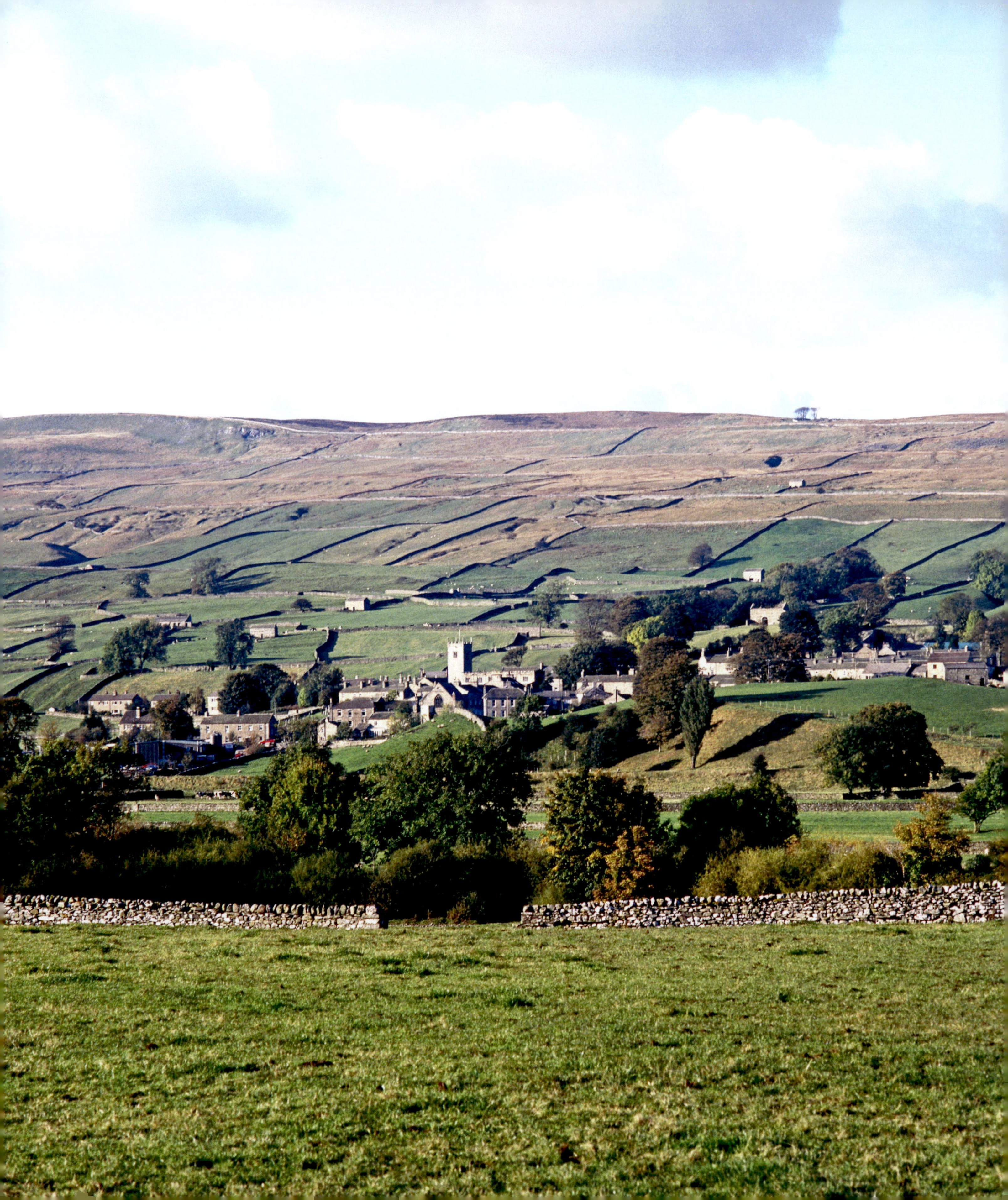

SCENES FROM HIS LIFE

Oswald Chambers, holding Kathleen, sits along a path in the Yorkshire moors with Mary Riley, a longtime friend through the League of Prayer and the Bible Training College. At the school, Mary Riley oversaw the "domestic students," those who handled kitchen and cleaning duties in exchange for their training; she would follow Oswald and Biddy to Egypt and devote herself to serving soldiers at the Y.M.C.A. camp. Years after Oswald Chambers's death, "Miss Riley" recalled both his teaching and example, saying "he had that lavish generosity which comes from a belief in a bountiful God. . . . Entirely free from possessions, he truly possessed all things."

OPPOSITE: The Yorkshire Dales village of Askrigg, where Oswald, Biddy, and Kathleen Chambers, along with several members of the "family"—both biological and from the Bible Training College—vacationed in August 1915. The parish church in the center is named, appropriately, St. Oswald's.

Bible Training College 113

SCENES FROM HIS LIFE

Oswald Chambers in Yorkshire: fishing, carrying Kathleen, and on a picnic with Biddy and his brother Arthur.

114 Oswald Chambers: A Life in Pictures

Bible Training College student Eva Spink wrote that she was one of the students "privileged to spend a part or whole of a holiday in Askrigg with Mr. and Mrs. Chambers and their little daughter Kathleen" in August 1915. "Here again was vouchsafed to us a fresh glimpse of this servant of God's spontaneous life; whether it was fishing or picnicking, or preaching in some wayside chapel, the evidence of the immense reality of his life with God was unmistakable. To use his own words, he was 'ever playing in God's presence as well as praying in it.' And how frequently praying he was, for never a walk or a picnic over those Yorkshire moors took place without his leading in a prayer of thanksgiving for the blessings of the day and a prayer for the men at the front, amongst whom he was so shortly going forth as a witness to join 'for the sake of the Name.' How significant was the verse in 2 Timothy 4:6 to which at the time he frequently referred as God's marching orders for him—'I am now ready to be offered, and the time of my departure is at hand.'"

A page from Eva Spink's B.T.C. notebook, with a heading that became the title of the February 5 and 6 entries of *My Utmost for His Highest*.

BELOW: Eva Spink in Egypt with British soldier Steven Pulford, her future husband. Pulford would accept Christ after the war while reading Oswald's *Studies in the Sermon on the Mount* and become a vicar in the Church of England.

Bible Training College

A 1916 photo of Y.M.C.A. secretaries and workers includes Oswald, Biddy, and Kathleen Chambers (seated in the first row) as well as Katherine Ashe, the B.T.C. student-turned-teacher who became part of the "expeditionary force" and worked in Alexandria (middle row, second from left).

9 THE Y.M.C.A. IN EGYPT

It was something of the nature of an earthquake to root up from London and the B.T.C., but where He leads we follow, and a joy it is, too. It is a great thing to be detached enough from possessions so as not to be held by them, because when called to uproot it is done with little real trouble.

OSWALD CHAMBERS, *diary entry, October 12, 1915*

Oswald Chambers confided in his diary that the Bible Training College had been "the Gate of Heaven" to him and Biddy. But God had "so profoundly called us out" that he could pursue his next spiritual assignment without regret. "It is wonderful that I am not home-sick for the B.T.C.," he wrote while en route to Egypt.

Had nostalgic feelings tried to arise, Chambers could take courage in the fact that his wife and daughter and several former pupils were planning to join him as soon as possible. "I have my sailing orders for Egypt for October 9th," he wrote to his mother on September 25, 1915. "I go first to prepare the way for Biddy and the students, this seems to me to be best anyway."

As he had with the college, Chambers viewed his role with the Y.M.C.A.—that of spiritual advisor to hundreds of commonwealth soldiers—as an adventure in the haphazard. "I go to behold [God's] wonderful undertakings in landing, and in Egypt, and in the camps," Oswald journaled. "It is a great charm not to know, but just to see Him unfold His purposes."

Playing off military parlance, Oswald called his team "the B.T.C. Expeditionary Force." He was the vanguard, arriving in Cairo on Tuesday, October 26, 1915, and the next day scouting out his own headquarters—the Y.M.C.A. facility at the Australian and New Zealand forces' large Base Detail Camp at Zeitoun. By the weekend, he had already put his imprint on the work. "To-day being Sunday," he wrote, "I am having nothing sold in the hut. I was told this would not work, but the hut is crammed to overflowing, and more than one has expressed a sense of satisfaction about it."

"The hut," a barn-like structure large enough to accommodate four hundred men, was the center of the Y.M.C.A.'s effort to provide wholesome activities for soldiers training nearby. Throughout the war zones of Europe and the Middle East, the organization offered writing materials, books, films, dances, athletic contests, lectures, and religious services for fighting men, hoping to shield them from such common temptations as alcohol and prostitution. For soldiers at Zeitoun, the danger was nearby Cairo, "like no other city on the earth for its allurements to vice," according to a history by Katherine Ashe.

Each camp's exact program varied by the individual "secretary" over it, and Oswald Chambers put Zeitoun's emphasis heavily on the spiritual. Just a week after his arrival, he held the first of many "talks"—lessons on biblical topics—that surprised other Y.M.C.A. secretaries by their popularity. "I have just talked to the men on 'What's the good of Prayer?'" Chambers wrote in his diary on November 4, 1915. "Thank God, the room was packed."

"In many ways Zeitoun was a unique Y.M.C.A. centre, because Mr. Chambers was a unique leader," Oswald's friend Gladys "Gladiolus" Donnithorne recalled after his death. "Shall we ever be able to forget those mighty meetings in the Devotional Hut? or some of the talks around the supper-table after the work of the day was over? or the blackboard hung in a prominent position announcing the evening meeting, with a daily thought written on it, such as—'Beware of anything that competes with loyalty to Jesus Christ,' or 'Be godly in the grubby details,' or 'When God says something never dispute, but do it'"?

118   Oswald Chambers: A Life in Pictures

In that initial lesson, Chambers taught that prayer doesn't so much change things as it changes the person who prays, so that he or she can then change things. It was a truth he had lived out himself, praying earnestly then "spending and being spent" for the soldiers.

And the men responded. Just days later, two "lads" accepted Christ and joined Oswald's War Roll, "a register in which men's names are put down as they come into the light." Many other conversions followed, as well as much spiritual growth, a fact that especially pleased Chambers. "Instruction is certainly the crying need among these men, and not the habitual evangelistic cry for Gospel meetings," he wrote in 1916. "There are so many 'saved' souls waiting instruction, and they take it with great zest."

Oswald respected the soldiers—"they are grand human stuff and stand up to anything that stands up to them," he said—and the military men reciprocated. Theodore Atkinson, a "well educated and sarcastic" Australian won to Christ through Chambers's influence, recalled,

Christianity was at a very low ebb in our camp when along came Oswald Chambers, with a positively unquenchable spirit alight in his face, a habit of taking the lowliest for himself, and a clear-cut personality that impressed one very much. I well remember his first night at the hut. His predecessor had found it necessary to plaster the walls with notices such as—"Please remember you are in a Y.M.C.A. hut and don't use bad language." . . . All those notices came down. It was never necessary to ask the men not to swear when Mr. Chambers was about.

Two soldiers, one with a cigarette, relax in bivouac in Egypt. Chambers personally avoided cigarettes, alcohol, and playing cards, but did not admonish those who used them. In his diary in October 1917, Oswald wrote of a soldier who had come to Christ and "lost all appetite for drink." Though the man found his smoking harder to give up, he ultimately "pitched his cigarette case over the wall and has never smoked since . . . just by the Spirit of God."

The Y.M.C.A. in Egypt

A camel, dressed for tourists, rests amid blowing sand outside Cairo. In May 1917, Oswald Chambers enjoyed the visit of a British army captain named Greenfield, stopping in Zeitoun after a six-month sojourn in Somaliland to purchase camels for the military. "He played our small organ and sang his Salvation Army hymns with great gusto," Chambers wrote in his diary. "It was a joy to see him enjoy himself!"

Describing Oswald's personality as "magnetic," a Y.M.C.A. official in Cairo said, "There was no effeminacy in his religion; he had a strong and virile faith. . . . He could enjoy to the full a talk with a lad about the highest things of life, he could also enjoy a discussion about practical things."

The practical things of Zeitoun included maddening insects, searing heat, blinding sandstorms, even the occasional torrential downpour. (During one storm, Chambers posted a sign saying the hut was "Closed during submarine manoeuvres!") Though he enjoyed some privileges the soldiers did not—Biddy and Kathleen were able to join him just after Christmas 1915, and he built his family a private home called "the Bungalow"— Oswald endured most of the hardships the men did.

Perhaps the worst aspect of camp life was the monotonous routine, the weeks and months of training in harsh "surroundings that never changed," as Katherine Ashe wrote. "Few people know, unless they have experienced it, what a climate such as that of Egypt can mean. . . . [It] is psychically appalling to certain temperaments, and to those who are spared this, there is yet the continual sapping of the physical forces by fever, and the resultant lowness of par which makes it difficult to fight moral or mental battles."

In one talk to the soldiers, Chambers said, "Everyone's soul represents some kind of battlefield. The point for each one is whether we will hang in, as Job did, and say 'Though things look black, I will trust in God.'" For the next two years, he engaged the moral and mental enemy with his men, serving as a spiritual commander, quartermaster, and medic.

A full century after, we know much of what Oswald Chambers said to the soldiers—his words were captured in Biddy's stenographic notebooks and ultimately published in volumes such as *Baffled to Fight Better*, *Facing Reality*, *Biblical Ethics*, *Conformed to His Image*, and *He Shall Glorify Me*. Men came out, often in large numbers, to hear his talks, with titles like "What Must I Believe to Be a Christian?," "Irresistible Discipleship," and "If God Is Love—Why?"

Years later, one soldier remembered the talk "Religious Problems Raised by the War," saying, "these words in bold letters on a board at the entrance to the [Egypt General Mission] Compound, in which the Y.M.C.A. at Zeitoun had its being, could not fail to arouse interest." He attended that lecture and many others to follow, ultimately accepting Christ in the postwar years as he read his Bible along with Oswald's *Studies in the Sermon on the Mount*.

Chambers began teaching the Sermon on the Mount at Zeitoun on a Monday evening in February 1916. "The attention is growing ever, and the keenness for Bible instruction is just great," he wrote in his diary. "The men are all sorts, divinity students, teachers, farmers, doctors; and the eagerness they show in crowding round afterward with their questions and eager thirst for Bible knowledge exceeds anything I have ever known."

As a teacher and preacher, Chambers seemed inexhaustible. He spoke daily at Zeitoun, and regularly at Cairo's Ezbekieh Gardens and the Aotea Convalescent Home, which was close enough for him to "saunter" over the desert sands. He often visited other camps and medical facilities throughout Egypt, sharing biblical wisdom in each. On Sundays, Katherine Ashe recalled, "it was not unusual for Oswald Chambers to have four services."

"Every night would see him at the work which he loved and excelled in—expounding the Scriptures in a masterly way to the men who gathered to hear him," friend and coworker Jimmy Hanson wrote for *Oswald Chambers: His Life and Work*. "Not only did they listen to the Scriptures being expounded by a real teacher, but they saw the life of which he spoke lived out before them. As one man put it to me—'If a man says he believes the New Testament, then the only outcome of his belief is that he lives as Oswald Chambers does.'"

The Y.M.C.A. in Egypt

Though Oswald taught crowds, he was also involved in soldiers' lives in personal ways. The Chambers home, the Bungalow, was a center of small group and one-on-one ministry, as Katherine Ashe described:

Here came many, many men, and in a daily intercourse filled with the simplicity of the common things of the common day lived in the Light, playing with Kathleen—jesting and light of heart—bringing and borrowing and talking books—or coming burdened and embittered and filled with such questioning as no other human soul can share—they touched always, whether in the lighter or the deeper things, the naked Reality of God.

The soldiers adored Kathleen, and gave her pets (such as a small donkey and other small animals), stole into the Bungalow to kiss her good night, even composed poems in her honor. One poet was Geoffrey Cumine, a combat engineer who trained at Zeitoun on his way to Gallipoli. Multi-published after the war, he was called a "rare mental comrade" by Katherine Ashe, "bohemian" and "eccentric" by later historians. His words indicate the ministry that even Oswald's young daughter had with the men:

*. . . as she shyly smiles
And lisps a little prayer because she's sure
That Someone hears and knows and
   understands,
Well, she's so pure,
So certain—that I wonder.*

Oswald Chambers, in the words of the Y.M.C.A.'s Stanley Barling, "was always a refreshment," but when Biddy and Kathleen arrived in Egypt, "the Y.M.C.A. at Zeitoun was a home in every sense of the word. Simplicity, yes, but a very centre of the milk of human kindness."

Biddy, too, enhanced Oswald's ministry by her hospitality at the Bungalow and through elaborate teas held in the huts. These popular Sunday afternoon events, free to the soldiers, were overseen by Biddy, Mary Riley, and other B.T.C. women, who provided a "touch of home" with drinks and desserts. The women always decorated each table with a white cloth and fresh flowers.

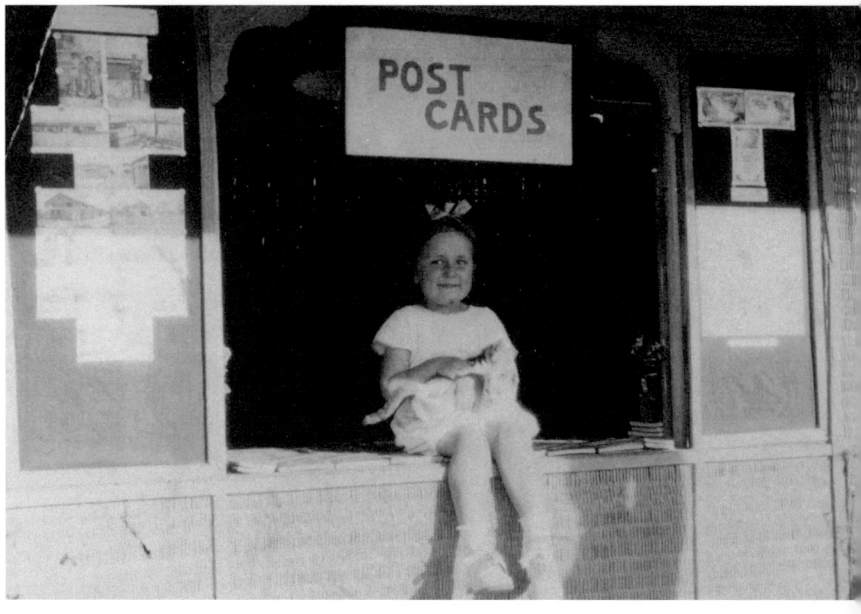

Oswald Chambers stands at the door of Zeitoun's "devotional hut." The photo, from later in the war, shows the additional buildings and landscaping that Chambers had supervised. "He spared no pains to make the place attractive so that it might minister comfort to the men," his friend Jimmy Hanson said.

The teas were indicative of Oswald's approach to ministry. He loved to teach, but he also labored to ensure that the soldiers' surroundings were as comfortable and interesting as possible. On May 3, 1917, he journaled that he'd spent much of the morning "doing little things in the huts," since he felt that a stagnant environment led to less attentive soldiers. "A grave defect in much work of to-day," Chambers wrote, "is that men do not follow Solomon's admonition, 'Whatsoever thy hand findeth to do, do it with thy might.' The tendency is to argue—'It's only for so short a time, why trouble?' If it is only for five minutes, let it be well done."

A Jerusalem minister who knew Oswald described him as "always busy but never flurried," and noted his wide-ranging capabilities—from meeting spiritual needs to managing the construction of buildings, such as a Y.M.C.A. hut at Ismailia. Chambers was reassigned there for several weeks in 1916, after every soldier was shipped out of Zeitoun. The transfer separated him from his family for almost a month, until military officials permitted Biddy and Kathleen to join him in a location much closer to the fighting front.

Over two years, Oswald visited every corner of Egypt. He ministered in several facilities around Cairo—Heliopolis, Gizeh, "the Aerodrome," and "the Racecourse," plus Bulac and Abassia hospitals—as well as farther-flung places like Alexandria, Port Said, Fayoum, Wardan, and Suez. In early 1917, he was "ruminating" on a return to England, but the Y.M.C.A. committee asked him to stay in Egypt. "This needs praying about," he wrote in his diary, "but we shall see it all right when the time comes."

The Y.M.C.A. in Egypt

By late February, Oswald was planning to send—not carry—photos of the compound to England for friends, "who by prayer and money helped to build the bungalow." He would continue to work with the soldiers as he had for the previous fifteen months.

Headquartered once again at Zeitoun, where military officials had opened a new "School of Instruction" the previous fall, Chambers kept preaching and teaching many times a week, all around Cairo and as far away as Alexandria. He managed construction of a new "information hut" and an underground study called the Dugout, designed for days like May 22, when the temperature reached 106 degrees in the shade. Four days earlier, during a howling sandstorm, he admitted "to-day is awful. . . . We eat sand, drink sand, think sand, and pray sand."

The ongoing burden of the Egyptian climate, his own physical exertion, and the soldiers' spiritual need was aging Oswald Chambers. A rare close-up photo from the time shows his face lined and gaunt, his piercing eyes less sparkling. On July 24, he marked his forty-third birthday.

In an uncharacteristic "out burst" (Oswald's own phrasing), a September 4 letter shows that the self-sacrificing servant longed to return to England. "Coming home!" he wrote to his brother Franklin, "what a day that will be, back to the cool and the cold, back to the mountains and the streams, back to the sea and the wee greatness of Britain. Why my very being is like a fountain of possible tears at the thought." He and Biddy were both "like an aching child for its mother's lap." But a return was not to be.

Oswald Chambers, after two years of hard work in a harsh environment, appearing much older than when he'd left the Bible Training College. "I see him in the heat of the day, denying himself the rest that was his due," a fellow worker recalled years later, "coming out to a canvas hospital on a visit to someone laid aside."

124   Oswald Chambers: A Life in Pictures

In late July 1917, the Chambers family had begun a brief vacation at Damietta and Ras el-Bar, on the Mediterranean coast, where Oswald wrote of "the sheer indolence of enjoyment." A few weeks later, he was reviewing printer's pages of *Baffled to Fight Better*, and in late September he got the "welcome news" that he should prepare to follow troops "up the line" for their campaign in Palestine.

During this time, Oswald gave a talk with a strange title that in hindsight seems a foreshadowing of his own death. The August 26 message at Aotea, based on Jeremiah 8:11, was called "A Poetical View of Appendicitis." Seven weeks later, on October 17, Chambers suffered an attack of that very condition.

It was not immediately diagnosed, and he tried at first to maintain his normal schedule. Soon, however, Oswald had to ask others to teach for him. Over the next several days, though clearly unwell, he mentioned in his diary only a "lack of opportunity for writing." With the army so near to battle, he resisted taking a hospital bed.

But by October 29—two years and a day after starting the work at Zeitoun—intense pain forced Chambers into the Red Cross hospital at Gizeh. An emergency appendectomy was performed, with apparent success—though in following days, complications from a blood clot in his lung proved fatal.

On November 15, 1917, Oswald Chambers slipped out of this life, going home to heaven rather than back to Britain. Stunned, hundreds of soldiers, coworkers, friends, and family members were left to ponder their own loss—and the apparent end of a powerful ministry.

———◇———

A military escort, rifles reversed in the traditional show of respect, marches past the wall of the Old Cairo cemetery to honor their beloved O.C.—the "officer in charge," Oswald Chambers.

The Y.M.C.A. in Egypt

EGYPT

Alexandria — Sidi Gaber ②⑫

Oswald and Biddy on a beach near Alexandria, Egypt.

Oswald aboard a felucca at Damietta

Ras el-Bar ⑦
Damietta ⑥

Nile R.

ABBASSIA DERMATOLOGICAL HOSPITAL ①
⑩ MOASCAR CAMP

④ Belbeis

⑭ Wardan

Oswald holds Kathleen at Giza, second from left

ZEITOUN
⑮ ③ AOTEA CONVALESCENT HOME
⑧ ⑤
Giza (Gizeh) Cairo

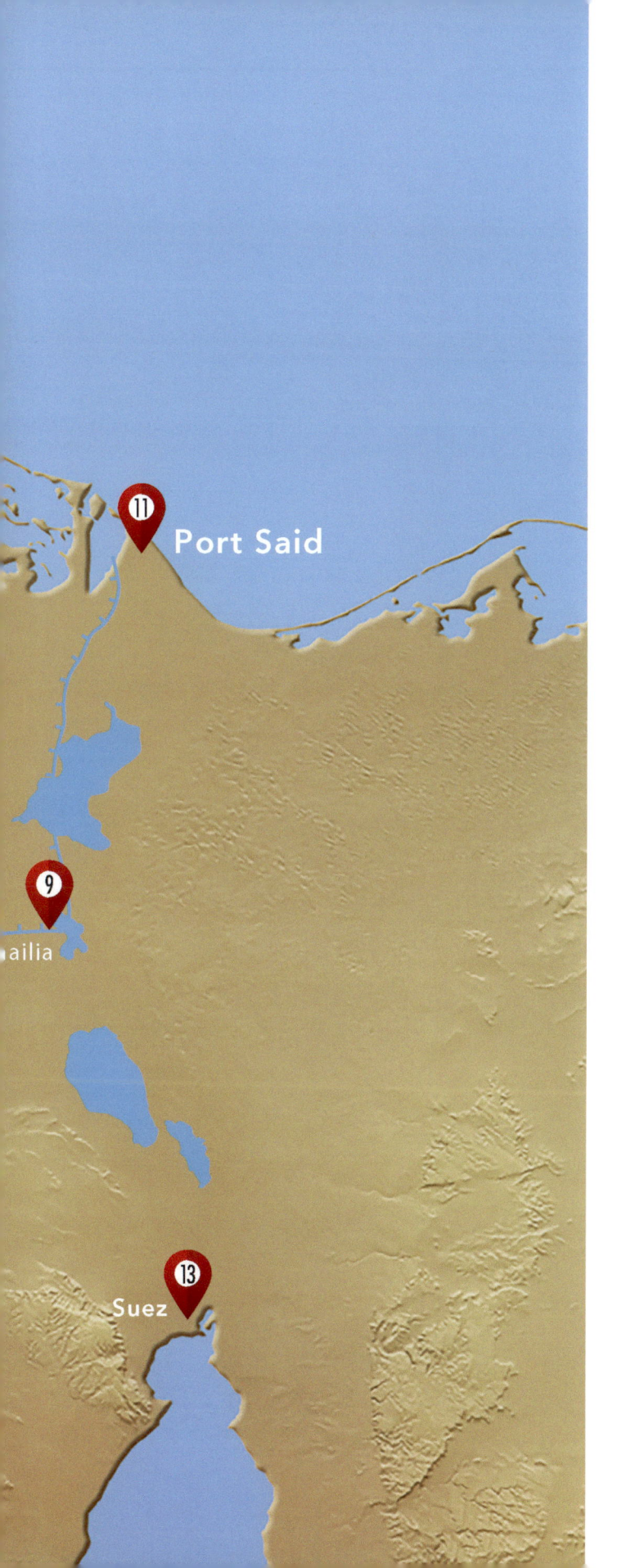

OSWALD CHAMBERS'S EGYPT, 1915–1917

1. **ABBASSIA DERMATOLOGICAL HOSPITAL:** Medical facility for Australian venereal patients; though military leadership treated these men as criminals, Chambers visited here shortly after arriving in Egypt, November 1915, and began a series of talks in late May 1917. "I am glad of the opportunity to talk to these men, many of them down and out in grosser sin, of the salvation and healing presence of Jesus Christ," he wrote in his diary.

2. **ALEXANDRIA:** Port city where Oswald arrived in Egypt and often led classes; the Chambers family vacationed here in April 1917, and Oswald attended his first church service in nineteen months.

3. **AOTEA CONVALESCENT HOME:** Facility in Heliopolis for ill and wounded New Zealand soldiers no longer needing hospitalization but not yet ready for military camp life; Oswald held regular Sunday morning services here, walking from Zeitoun.

4. **BELBEIS:** City where Kathleen spent a few days with missionary friends in October 1917; Oswald and Biddy traveled here to retrieve her just four days before his appendicitis attack.

5. **CAIRO:** Egyptian capital, approximately six miles from Zeitoun camp; location of Ezbekieh Gardens, where Oswald regularly held classes.

6, 7. **DAMIETTA, RAS EL-BAR:** Mediterranean cities where Oswald vacationed in late July and early August 1917.

8. **GIZA (GIZEH):** Site of pyramids and the sphinx; Oswald visited on at least four occasions and spoke at the nearby Australian camp in March 1916; he died in a Red Cross hospital here.

9. **ISMAILIA:** City along the Suez Canal that Oswald often visited; he was assigned here for a few months in 1916 when all soldiers were transferred out of Zeitoun.

10. **MOASCAR CAMP:** Oswald conducted an evangelistic mission here in late March 1916.

11. **PORT SAID:** Mediterranean port through which Biddy and Kathleen arrived in Egypt.

12. **SIDI GABER:** Neighborhood of Alexandria where Katherine Ashe worked with the Y.M.C.A.; Oswald led classes here on several occasions.

13. **SUEZ:** Oswald led evangelistic services here for "Tommies" (troops of the home island) in late March 1916.

14. **WARDAN:** Oswald led evangelistic services here for Tommies in late March 1916.

15. **ZEITOUN:** Oswald's headquarters during the war; he visited for the first time on October 27, 1915, beginning work the next day.

SCENES FROM HIS LIFE

Above, the Y.M.C.A. facilities at Zeitoun in early 1917, photographed from the adjacent building of the Egypt General Mission. Oswald Chambers had found a single hut when he arrived in October 1915; in following months he built his family residence, the Bungalow (building at center) and added the "devotional hut" (second building from the left). In the summer of 1917, he would install an underground study called the Dugout; at the time of this photo, he used the tepee-like bell tent as a study. At right, soldiers write letters inside the main hut at Zeitoun.

128   Oswald Chambers: A Life in Pictures

The Chambers family "kept open house for us all," said Theodore Atkinson, the Australian soldier who accepted Christ under Oswald's ministry. "Whatever they had they shared, and with little Kathleen running around and attending the Sunday services where she lustily sang the hymns, and Miss Riley's cooking, we began to feel almost as if we were home again." The picture of Oswald and Biddy in front of the lattice is from the summer of 1917, one of the last photographs taken of the couple.

The Y.M.C.A. in Egypt 129

SCENES FROM HIS LIFE

Loved as he was by the soldiers, Oswald Chambers's ministry was "greatly enriched by his wife and child," wrote a New Zealander, Guy Morton. The Australian Theodore Atkinson said "things got better and better" when Biddy and Kathleen arrived in Egypt. "What a wonderful family it was," said another Australian, Stuart Gardiner, "and how splendidly all its members radiated Christian service in that vast Camp on the desert's edge!"

130   Oswald Chambers: A Life in Pictures

"I have a picture of Kathleen before me—just a 'snap' taken one morning in 1917 on the Bungalow verandah," Katherine Ashe wrote in *The Book of the Bungalow*. "Her father came behind and lifted her topee and the light has caught her face—such radiance of a perfectly simple, happy child, caught at her playing with Love all about her." The little girl's "happy laughter and winsome ways," Stuart Gardiner recalled, "made her a child beloved, daily adding to her court of devoted admirers, and touching with her wee hands the vibrant chords of father love that made melody in the hearts of men long separated from their little ones."

The Y.M.C.A. in Egypt

SCENES FROM HIS LIFE

The Chambers' friend Jimmy Hanson, a one-time Bible Training College student who followed Oswald into Y.M.C.A. work in Egypt, described the family's wartime living conditions as "extraordinary." And yet, in the midst of a world conflict and surrounded by soldiers coming from and going into battle, Chambers made time for some small pleasures for himself and his "family"—Biddy and Kathleen, as well as the B.T.C. Expeditionary Force.

Oswald and Kathleen at the beach; father and daughter with a pet donkey, compliments of Peter Kay.

132   Oswald Chambers: A Life in Pictures

Above, a picnic in the desert; at left, Oswald with dogs, one of his great joys in life. "He had this tremendous delight in children, and tremendous delight in dogs—he loved dogs," Kathleen recalled decades later. Her father, she said, had "an overpowering sense of delight in living, and an incredibly deep knowledge of God."

The Y.M.C.A. in Egypt 133

SCENES FROM HIS LIFE

Oswald Chambers went to Egypt under the auspices of the Young Men's Christian Association, an organization that began in London in 1844 and rapidly spread around the globe. During the first world war, the Y.M.C.A. set up some four thousand huts for soldiers' use—including numerous facilities around Cairo, Egypt, under the supervision of an American, William Jessop. "He and his wife are out and out people of God," Chambers wrote in his diary.

Stanley Barling, "a very fine Christian lad," welcomed Oswald to Cairo, and became "an ever welcome guest" in the Chambers home. After Chambers's funeral, Barling wrote, "Words of real testimony were given by different ones of how, when groping in the dark, Mr. Chambers had guided them to Jesus Christ. Their testimonies were only a sample of what might be given by hundreds of our fighting men."

Chambers and Stanley Barling in a Y.M.C.A. portrait. Compare Oswald's appearance in this 1915 photo with the picture on page 124, taken two years later.

134   Oswald Chambers: A Life in Pictures

Ernest Nickson, a vicar in northern England after the war, recalled that Bible studies typically began with soldiers trying to "elucidate the contents of the blackboard which is prepared ready for the lecture. Alliteration is here to perfection. Each heading of the Study is crisp and clear, vitally connected with subsequent sub-headings, each sub-heading an essential part of what proceeds, completing the scheme of reasoning. But Philip's question to the eunuch is apposite: 'Understandest thou what thou readest?' And every soldier shakes a perplexed head, and says: 'How can I, except some man should guide me?'"

That man was "the personification of the Sherlock Holmes of fiction, tall, erect, virile, with clean-cut face, framing a pair of piercing bright eyes. One feels instinctively that here is a detective of the soul, one who has been in intimate fellowship with the unseen and can now speak with calm assurance of eternal things." Oswald Chambers, speaking in a "crisp staccato voice," opened each session in prayer with pleas like, "We ask that Thou wilt make it easy for us to worship Thee."

Stuart Gardiner recalled, "The men who listened to these memorable talks of the O.C.'s returned again to the Line—to its danger and hardship—treasuring the possession of their Bibles, for his words had been like the penetrating rays of a great light which had lit up the darkness of their ignorance and indifference, and brought them face to face with the only thing that mattered—their relationship to God."

The Chambers family, with Oswald holding an easel. He used a blackboard both to advertise his Bible studies and to give the men a memorable visual outline of his lectures.

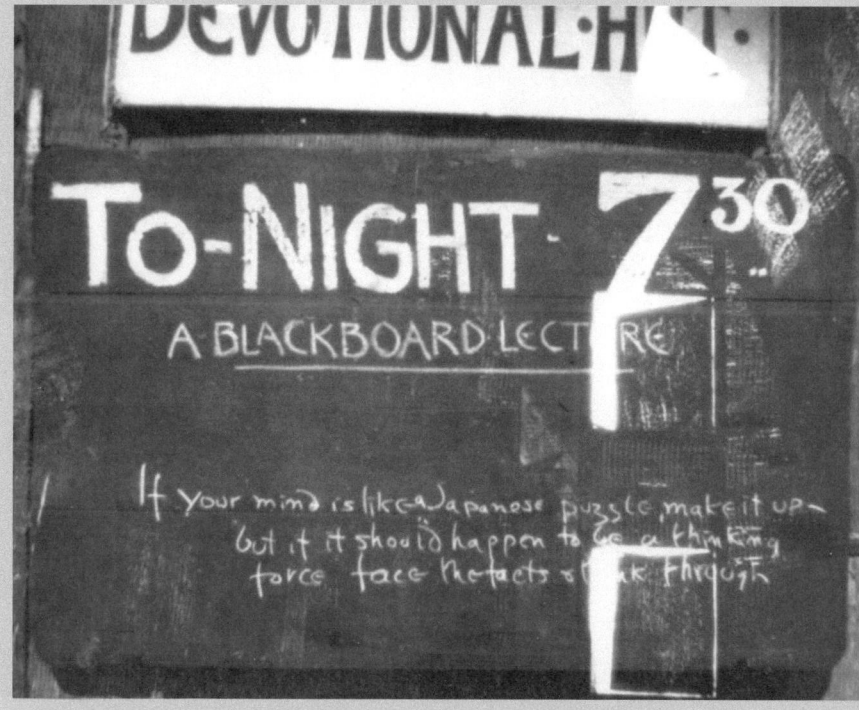

The Y.M.C.A. in Egypt 135

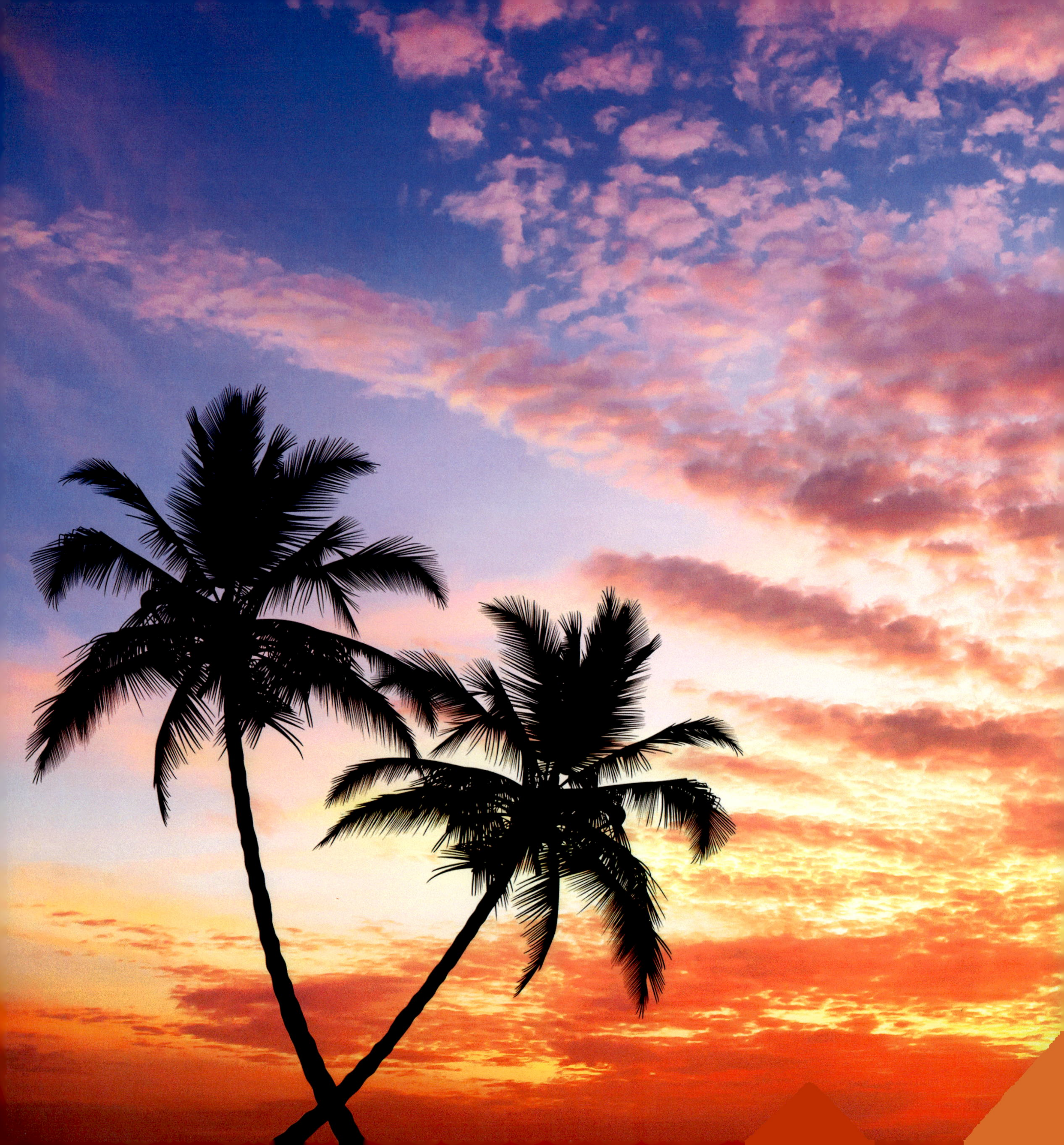

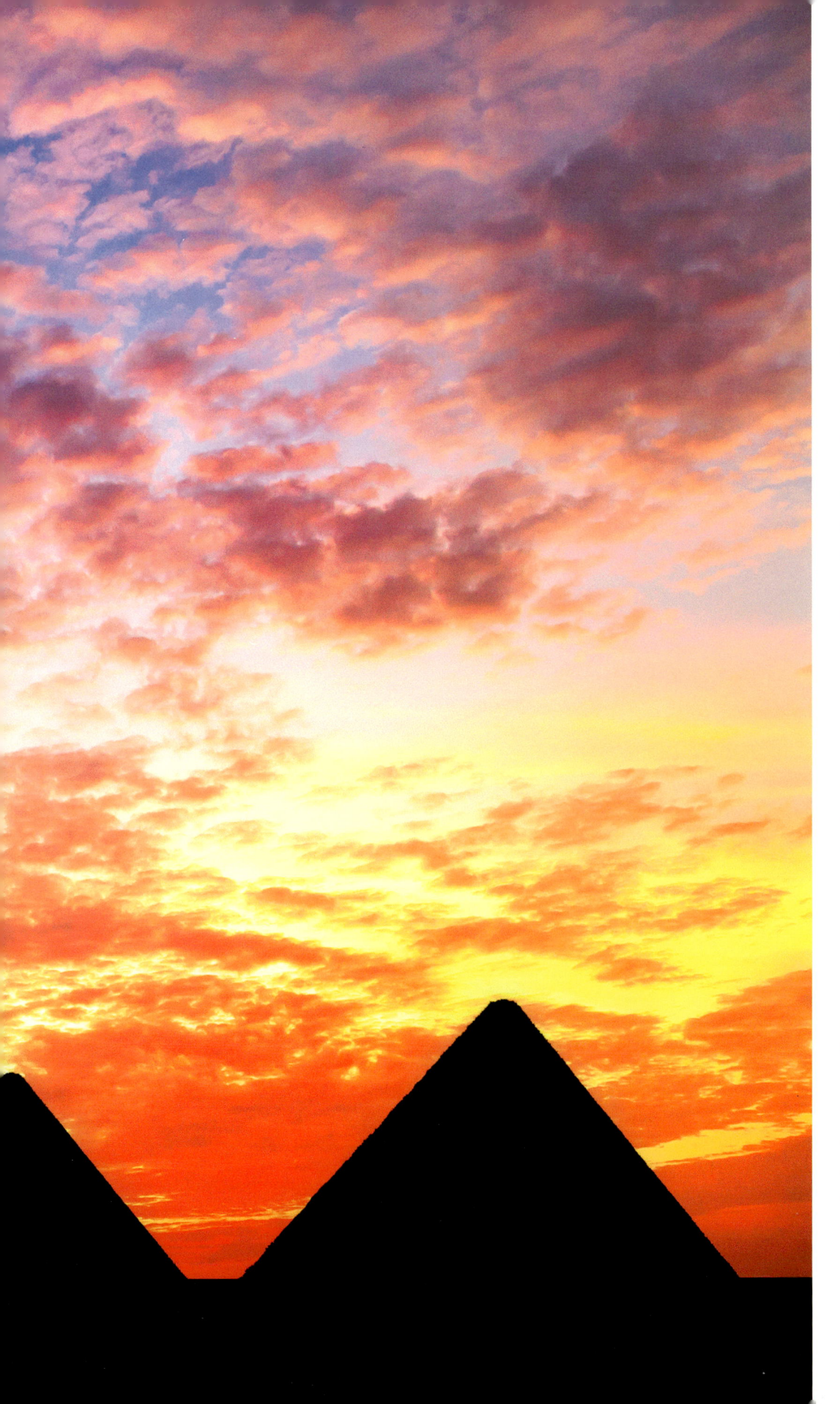

Egypt's daytime sun could be, in Oswald Chambers's phrasing, "an unveiled scorcher," but he marveled at the desert's sunrises and sunsets. "These mornings!" he wrote on October 14, 1916. "This morning it is like the merry heart of God's home beaming generous love all over the earth." On October 30, 1916: "A pure chalice of God's elixir—that comes near an indication of the rare beauty of the dawn and early morning." On February 24, 1917: "The gates of the West were silently transfigured and the glory as of God simply flooded the world before the healing loveliness of the Eastern night folded everything in a blissful darkness, radiant with stars." On May 21, 1917: "What an inexhaustibly beautiful mind our Lord must have!"

Katherine Ashe, commenting on the emotional hardships soldiers faced in the desert, wrote, "Many were saved mentally by one thing—the beauty and the eternal freshness of the Desert sunsets and dawns."

SCENES FROM HIS LIFE

"The Dugout" was one of Oswald's building projects at Zeitoun. A late addition to the compound, the below-ground-level study was designed to shield Oswald and Biddy from the desert's oppressive heat. "What transpires in that dugout, while we are marching and drilling and instructing the troops on the parade grounds?" asked Ernest Nickson. "The Lord Jesus Himself and Oswald Chambers knew. He had held such communion with his Saviour that the dugout has become the house of God to him, and he makes us long to grow in grace and knowledge that we may assimilate the 'strong meat' he puts before us."

Clockwise from top right, Oswald overseeing the excavation of the Dugout; standing beside the partially-built structure; an interior view of his work space; and the Chambers family, enjoying the shade in front of the building.

138   Oswald Chambers: A Life in Pictures

John Blight, an Australian soldier, summarized Chambers's ministry in Egypt in a long letter published in *Oswald Chambers: His Life and Work*. He wrote,

> A military camp is the last place to which one would willingly go for influences that touch the finer side of life and that speak of things that are age-abiding; but at the Y.M.C.A. hut at Ismailia, in spite of the hampering influences of militarism, men were brought face to face with a greater reality than the grim reality of war. The memory of days spent with Oswald Chambers in Egypt surpasses in vividness all other memories, and eclipses the physical and mental nausea and discomfort of the campaign. From that time life could never be the same again.
>
> As a member of the A.I.F. [Australian Imperial Force], I found myself amongst those stationed at Ismailia after the evacuation of Gallipoli. Immediately upon our arrival I sought out the Y.M.C.A. hut. . . . Of the hut at Ismailia I can now remember very little. I suppose that hut ministered to my creature needs, but that has left no impress upon my mind; this one thing I do know—that there I met a man, and because of that, that hut stands out more vividly in my memory than any other place visited during the long four and a half years. This keen-faced, lean and alert man, this man with a thousand tasks, but with no suggestion ever of hustle or weariness, was the greatest man I have ever met. Here, one felt was a prophet, a teacher, a disciple of Jesus Christ. . . .
>
> His was no semi-religious work, but a straight-out spiritual appeal. He never adopted the "For soldiers only" attitude. His approach to the "digger" was the same as to an ordinary citizen. He required much of those with whom he came in close contact . . . ethical, moral and spiritual obligations were in no wise whittled down. If attending his classes, one was required to have one's mind at the utmost attention. How well I remember him saying—"Don't be afraid of a headache, it is evidence that you have some brains."
>
> Mr. Chambers' mode of attack was never dulled by familiarity with his subject. How violently we at times disagreed with some of his utterances, and how eagerly he welcomed our disagreement; but as the days went by we found ourselves dimly appreciating things as he taught them. In those days we were up against the bare nakedness of things and learned above all else to appreciate reality. Can any wonder then that we appreciated Oswald Chambers?

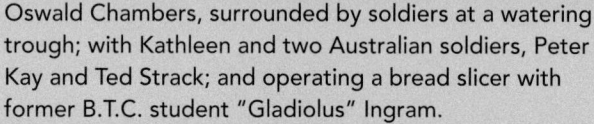

SCENES FROM HIS LIFE

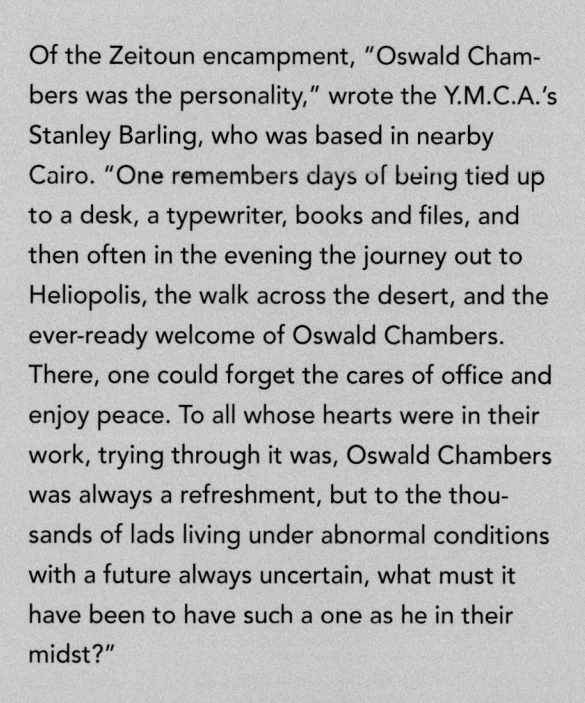

Oswald Chambers, surrounded by soldiers at a watering trough; with Kathleen and two Australian soldiers, Peter Kay and Ted Strack; and operating a bread slicer with former B.T.C. student "Gladiolus" Ingram.

Of the Zeitoun encampment, "Oswald Chambers was the personality," wrote the Y.M.C.A.'s Stanley Barling, who was based in nearby Cairo. "One remembers days of being tied up to a desk, a typewriter, books and files, and then often in the evening the journey out to Heliopolis, the walk across the desert, and the ever-ready welcome of Oswald Chambers. There, one could forget the cares of office and enjoy peace. To all whose hearts were in their work, trying through it was, Oswald Chambers was always a refreshment, but to the thousands of lads living under abnormal conditions with a future always uncertain, what must it have been to have such a one as he in their midst?"

140   Oswald Chambers: A Life in Pictures

Long before email, texting, or common use of the telephone, telegrams (called "cables" when sent via underwater lines) were the quickest way to share news—but their expense encouraged very concise messages. "Oswald in His Presence" was the first word of Chambers's death sent to his parents, his brothers Arthur and Franklin, Biddy's mother and sister, and the League of Prayer's Mrs. Reader Harris, who would then inform other friends and relatives. In time, slightly more information was provided via this card.

After Oswald's death, Jim Skidmore—a "greatly loved friend" and brother of the League of Prayer's John Skidmore—wrote Biddy to say, "We approach this phase of the mystery of His will with awe, and as we confess the narrow limits of our comprehension, we realize more fully how unsearchable are His judgments and His ways past finding out. . . . We take courage and feel that He is permitting us to enter into fellowship with His sufferings. In the mighty conflict that is now being waged between God and Satan there are more important fronts than the merely visible ones, and the Lord needs generals of His grace in the heavenlies as much as, or more than, on the earth."

The Y.M.C.A. in Egypt

SCENES FROM HIS LIFE

Oswald Chambers was a Y.M.C.A. secretary, a volunteer chaplain to British commonwealth troops—but when he died after two years of service, he was accorded full military honors and a spot among the soldiers in the Old Cairo cemetery.

In the photos opposite (top), soldiers carry Oswald Chambers's casket into the cemetery. In the image below, uniforms—both military and Y.M.C.A.—predominate as the dress of the mourners. Biddy Chambers biographer Michelle Ule identifies the white-haired man to the left, holding his hat, as Lord Radstock, a Y.M.C.A. official; immediately to his right, dressed in black, is Biddy.

This wooden cross originally marked Oswald Chambers's grave. The carved stone Bible was a gift of Peter Kay, and highlighted Oswald's beloved Luke 11:13.

The Y.M.C.A. in Egypt 143

Oswald Chambers's permanent gravestone, featuring the Y.M.C.A.'s triangle logo, identifies him as a superintendent with the organization but more importantly as "A believer in Jesus Christ." His remains lie among the British soldiers he served so faithfully from October 1915 to November 1917.

"It seemed hard to understand why God had allowed the work of such an inspired teacher to cease just at the time when its influence was so powerful and uplifting a force in so many lives," Stuart Gardiner wrote. Eventually, though, friends and relatives would begin to see that God was extending Oswald Chambers's ministry far beyond this particular time and place.

REVEREND
OSWALD CHAMBERS
SUPERINTENDENT Y.M.C.A.
15TH NOVEMBER 1917 AGE 43

A BELIEVER IN JESUS CHRIST

The typewriter and Bible that Biddy Chambers used while converting her notes of Oswald's spoken lessons into pamphlets and books. "It is such a blessing that you were able to preserve those valuable talks and publish them," a former soldier from New Zealand wrote, "for even here in this remote part of the world, I know those who are reading the books and being wonderfully helped by them."

10 HIS ONGOING MINISTRY

The final test and witness of spiritual force is the ability to cast the bodily life away and yet continue to give help and courage to those who see us no longer, to be, like Christ, the helper of men's souls—even from beyond the grave.

OSWALD CHAMBERS'S FRIEND "MICK" WARREN, *quoting Phillips Brooks*

Had Oswald Chambers never met Gertrude Hobbs, he would still have been a powerful preacher and teacher. But, a hundred years after his death, he would probably be little remembered, and almost certainly not known for the dozens of books that now carry his name.

Within weeks of his "entering into Life," as Biddy described it, Oswald's ongoing ministry—the written word—took the form of a leaflet sermon for soldiers they'd met over the preceding two years. Many were writing to express grief and condolence over "the O.C.'s" death.

As the holidays neared, the Chambers' friend and coworker Jimmy Hanson approached Biddy with a scrapbook of Oswald's teaching, clipped from the League of Prayer's magazine. Hanson highlighted "The Place of Help," the article on which the newlyweds had collaborated in 1910. "Wouldn't it be a fine message to send to the men for Christmas?" he asked.

Biddy agreed, quickly preparing a version to be printed and sent out "far and wide," she recalled years later. The response was immediate, with requests for more—so Biddy began sending one of Oswald's talks each month, a new ministry birthed "in the seemingly haphazard way in which God's order comes, as we had so often been taught."

Though the Y.M.C.A. soon took responsibility for the distribution of the sermons, shipping ten thousand copies a month to every camp in Egypt, Palestine, and France, Biddy kept the preparation of the text as part of her regular work—continuing Oswald's service to the troops around Cairo.

Immediately after her husband's funeral, Biddy left for a week at the Nile River city of Luxor, some four hundred miles south of Zeitoun, staying with an American missionary family on their ministry boat. She traveled with Kathleen and the B.T.C.'s Eva Spink (whom Oswald had nicknamed "Sphinx"), and on their way back north the group spent a second week with other friends-of-friends in Wasta, Egypt. Biddy returned to work at Zeitoun on November 30, only fifteen days after Oswald's death.

William Jessop, the Y.M.C.A. director at Cairo, had asked Biddy to carry on with Oswald's ministry, "and while there was never any doubt about the answer," she recalled, "there was an unspoken doubt as to whether there could possibly be a manifestation of the same radiant spirit which had made life so full of joy to us all." Ultimately, Biddy learned by experience the truth of 2 Corinthians 12:9, that God's grace would be sufficient. "We became very conscious, too," she recalled, "that though [Oswald was] 'absent in the flesh,' he was very 'present in the spirit.'"

Biddy would lead services and classes, often facilitating discussions of Oswald's material, such as his study of biblical psychology. The Sunday teas continued as well, but in and around these duties, she also began to assemble her late husband's teaching into books.

After Oswald's death, Biddy and Kathleen enjoyed a support team of friends from the B.T.C., Y.M.C.A., Egypt General Mission, and British military. At lower right in this photo is Jimmy Hanson, the Bible Training College student who followed Oswald into Y.M.C.A. work, and who suggested the first "leaflet" talk for distribution to the soldiers.

Biddy possessed a treasury of raw material. "It is hardly possible to pay adequate tribute to the devotion of Mrs. Chambers in recording [Oswald's] spoken words, full shorthand notes having been taken of lectures and sermons and addresses almost without exception," wrote C. Rae Griffin, a friend who assisted with publications. Before long, much larger projects augmented the simple leaflets for the soldiers; Oswald's first posthumous book was his study of redemption called *The Shadow of an Agony*, printed in 1918.

While Oswald was alive, a handful of books bore his name, including *Biblical Psychology* and *Studies in the Sermon on the Mount*, both published by God's Revivalist Press in Cincinnati, and a series of "Discipline" booklets released at the end of his B.T.C. years. In his final months, Oswald had worked with Biddy on *Baffled to Fight Better*, which became available in December 1917, just weeks after his death.

Though every volume contained Oswald's words, it is inaccurate to say that he "wrote books." As a preacher and teacher, he prepared and delivered messages—but Biddy took verbatim notes that *she* later assembled into books.

"I feel as if I will never come to an end of my wealth of notes," Biddy wrote to her sister, Dais, in 1918. Fifteen years later, while preparing the manuscript for *Oswald Chambers: His Life and Work*, she said, "From those first days until now a constant stream of messages has been sent out, and still my store of notes seems inexhaustible." This "work of the books" would continue for four decades and result in some four dozen separate volumes.

Biddy, photographed in Cairo in 1918 or 1919, and the title page spread of the first book she produced after Oswald's death. The content of *The Shadow of an Agony* was from some of the last talks he gave to soldiers in Zeitoun, in late August 1917.

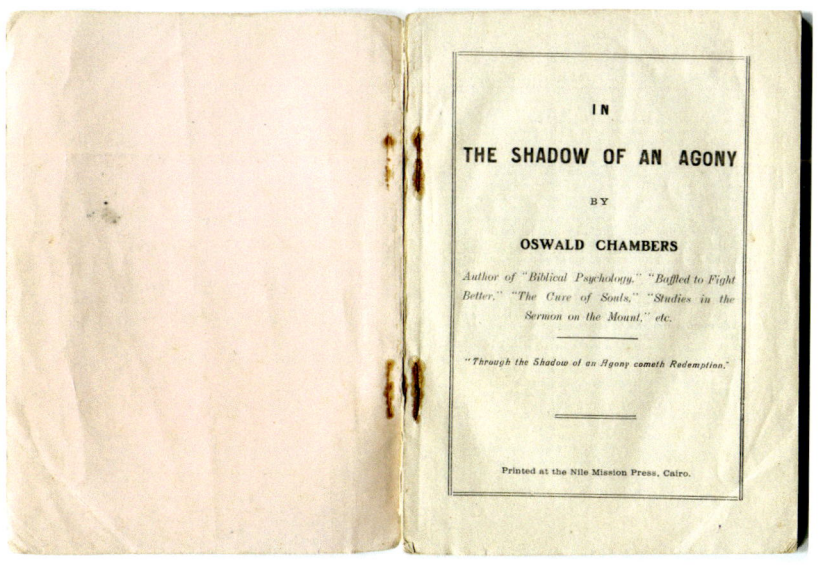

His Ongoing Ministry

Biddy Chambers captured Oswald's teaching in shorthand, a skill she developed during her teen years. "When Mother was a child of thirteen," Kathleen recalled, "she was unable to continue her schooling because of illness. She then undertook to master shorthand, with the ambition one day of becoming secretary to the Prime Minister. She reached the fantastic speed of 250 words a minute." The Pitman shorthand Biddy learned was used by court stenographers to record testimony verbatim.

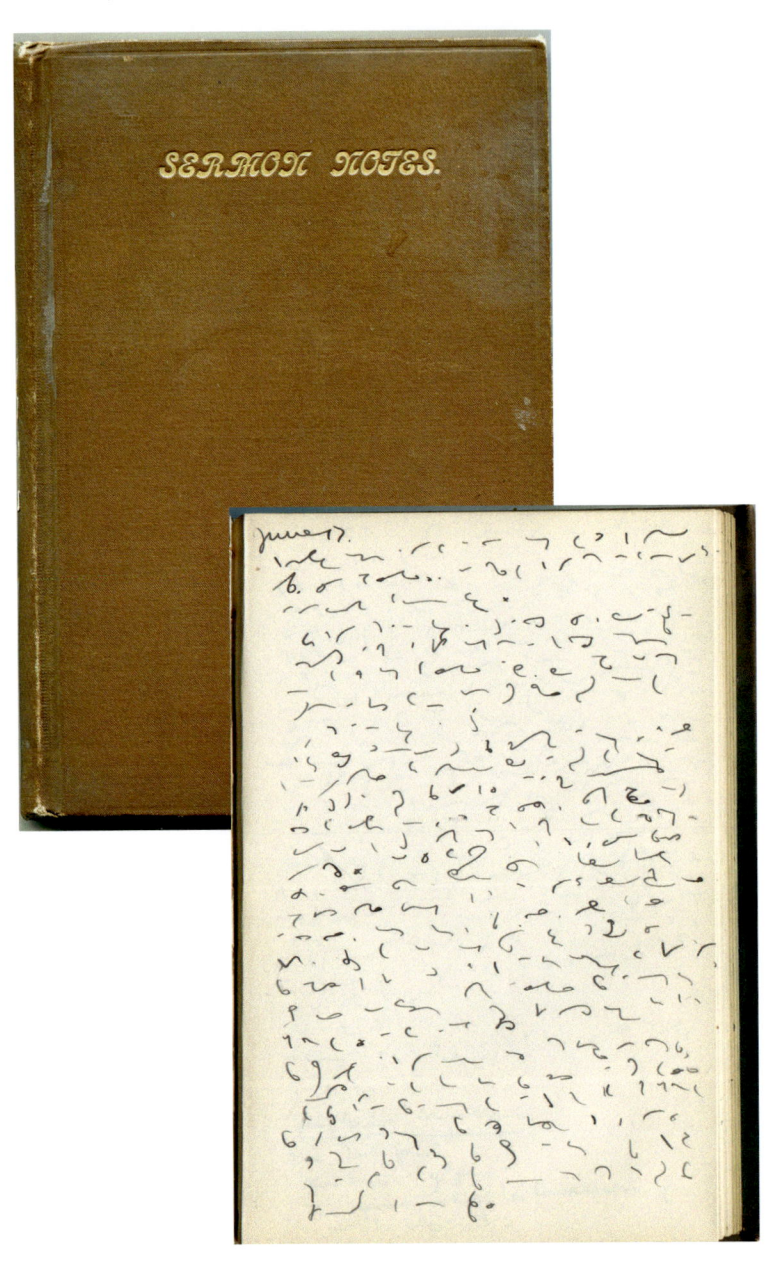

Biddy's work collating and editing seven years' worth of Oswald's teaching is remarkable, considering all her other responsibilities after his death—carrying on duties at Zeitoun, raising Kathleen singlehandedly, ultimately running a lodging house back in England. But she described the labor as "a joy and a privilege."

The return to England, an unfulfilled dream of Oswald's, happened for Biddy and Kathleen in early July 1919. The armistice ending the war had taken effect November 11, 1918, four days before the anniversary of Oswald's death. But Biddy and several of her colleagues stayed in Egypt for another eight months as British officials drew down the military forces in the region.

Once again in London, Biddy and Kathleen lived for a while with Emily and Dais Hobbs, then with a young family with League of Prayer and B.T.C. connections. In time, mother and daughter took a small, primitive cottage outside the ancient university town of Oxford. During these years, 1919–24, Biddy oversaw a British printing of *Biblical Psychology* and the publication of both *The Psychology of Redemption* and *The Shade of His Hand*.

When offered a large, reasonably priced house within Oxford, Biddy took it, along with the opportunity to earn rent from student boarders. For nearly three years, while she shopped, cooked, and cleaned for the lodgers, she also worked on the book that would become synonymous with the name Oswald Chambers: *My Utmost for His Highest*. It would be released in 1927 and become one of the world's best known, most loved devotionals.

In her foreword to *My Utmost*, Biddy Chambers quoted the revered Scottish minister Robert Murray McCheyne, who had died of typhus in 1843 at age twenty-nine: "Men return again and again to the few who have mastered the spiritual secret, whose life has been hid with Christ in God." Of her husband, another Scottish minister who lived a brief but powerful life, she wrote,

> *It is because it is felt that the author is one to whose teaching men will return, that this book has been prepared, and it is sent out with the prayer that day by day the messages may continue to bring the quickening life and inspiration of the Holy Spirit.*

"I think if I have an ambition," Oswald Chambers had once said, "it is that I might have honourable mention in anyone's personal relationship with Our Lord Jesus Christ." Over the following decades, his ambition and Biddy's prayer were accomplished in remarkable ways which show no signs of slowing in the second century after his death.

Oswald and Biddy Chambers both devoted themselves to God, who used the couple powerfully in His work. "We have to realise that no effort can be too high, because Jesus says we are to be the children of our Father in heaven," Oswald taught. "It must be my utmost for His highest all the time and every time."

"His religion had no room for sin, sham, sloth, or slovenliness in the Christian," said Eric Ofverberg, who with his wife took in Biddy and Kathleen in the early 1920s. "The fittest summary of the life and teaching of Oswald Chambers is perhaps the title of his best-known book—*My Utmost for His Highest*."

The Golden Book of Oswald Chambers

MY UTMOST FOR HIS HIGHEST

Selections for the Year

LONDON:
SIMPKIN MARSHALL, LTD.
STATIONERS' HALL COURT, E.C.4

His Ongoing Ministry

SCENES FROM HIS LIFE

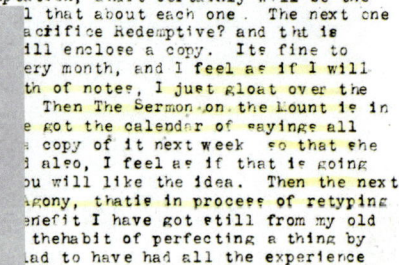

Eight months after Oswald's death, in an August 1918 letter to her sister, Biddy Chambers described several book projects she already had underway. She also noted that she was doing the work from the Dugout her husband had built at Zeitoun. "I begin to find it very true what Oswald always said, you infect the places you occupy, and they have a corresponding influence whenever you enter them," she wrote, "so I want to keep the dugout as an inspiration." The portrait of Biddy and Kathleen is from about 1921, when they had been back in England for two years. At the time, Biddy was around thirty-eight; Kathleen eight.

Biddy and Kathleen Chambers around 1927, the year of the British release of *My Utmost for His Highest*. It would be published in the United States in 1935 and ultimately become one of the most popular devotionals of all time.

Biddy compiled the 366 daily readings of *My Utmost* from Oswald's teaching at the Bible Training College and the Y.M.C.A. huts of Egypt. She followed the pattern of other famous devotionals, including *Daily Light on the Daily Path*, which Oswald and Biddy read regularly, and *Morning and Evening* by Charles H. Spurgeon, under whose ministry Oswald had been converted. Two years before *My Utmost* became available, *Streams in the Desert*—another daily devotional that remains popular today—was released by Lettie Cowman, a missionary who had studied at God's Bible School and welcomed Oswald to Japan in 1907.

My Utmost for His Highest was compiled over three years in Oxford, in the same time and place C. S. Lewis and J. R. R. Tolkien, recently appointed professors, were building their own teaching and writing careers.

An early Canadian edition of *My Utmost for His Highest*

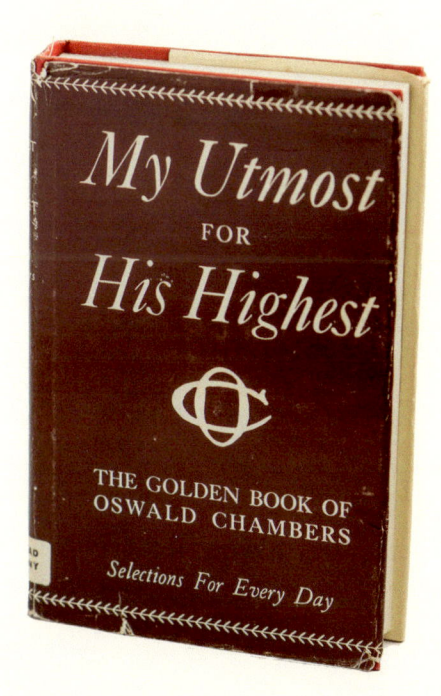

His Ongoing Ministry 153

SCENES FROM HIS LIFE

To help Biddy with the business aspect of the books, the Oswald Chambers Publications Association, a group of relatives, friends, and ministry partners, was incorporated in 1942—though the group had begun, in an unofficial capacity, more than twenty years before. Early on, the council included Biddy's mother, Emily Amelia Hobbs (1850–1934).

On the fiftieth anniversary of Oswald's death, one year after Biddy's passing in 1966, the association printed this pamphlet showing the thirty-two books then available. Oswald and Biddy's daughter, Kathleen, regularly attended every meeting of the Association from 1966 until her death, at age eighty-four, in 1997. The Oswald Chambers Publications Association Limited continues to this day, with four British and two American trustees, "to advance the Christian religion through the writings of the late Oswald Chambers."

He left this life more than a hundred years ago, but his ministry is ongoing. Biddy, as a widow for less than a week, had enjoyed a hint of the blessing that Oswald would be to future generations of Christians:

God brought to my mind the last words I heard my husband speak—"Greater works than these shall he do, because I go unto My Father" [John 14:12]. I felt as if God were there in Person by my side actually speaking the words to me, and instantly everything that had seemed to shut one in to the immediate present, lifted, and again there was "the land of far distances," and the assurance came, dimly at first, of a work yet to be done for Him. And always those so unfathomably profound words of our Lord's have been linked in thought and prayer with the books as they go forth.

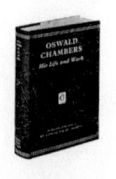

154 Oswald Chambers: A Life in Pictures

By the centennial of Oswald Chambers's death, the "work of the books" had touched millions of readers in countries around the world. *My Utmost for His Highest* had appeared in more than forty translations, including all the major languages (such as French, Spanish, German, and Chinese) as well as Afrikaans, Bulgarian, Greek, Hindi, Mongolian, and Swahili. The number of copies printed, spread over ninety years and numerous publishers, is difficult to quantify exactly, but a figure of more than twelve million can be documented. It is believed the actual total is considerably higher.

Tens of thousands of readers interact with *My Utmost* every day via electronic media—a website, email, an app, and multiple social media platforms. All of Chambers's books are available in a 1,492-page, single-volume "complete works" edition, and several individual titles remain in print as well.

Though Oswald Chambers had enthusiastically proposed a "literary" work to Biddy, he died with only a handful of books to his name. It is hard to believe he ever envisioned such a vast, ongoing worldwide ministry. Simple faithfulness was his watchword, as he wrote to his sister Florence in 1907:

> I want to tell you a growing conviction with me, and that is that as we obey the leadings of the Spirit of God, we enable God to answer the prayers of other people. I mean that our lives, my life, is the answer to someone's prayer, prayed perhaps centuries ago. It is more and more impossible to me to have programmes and plans because God alone has the plan, and our plans are only apt to hinder Him and make it necessary to Him to break them up. I have the unspeakable knowledge that my life is the answer to prayers, and that God is blessing me and making me a blessing entirely of His sovereign grace and nothing to do with my merits, saving as I am bold enough to trust His leading and not the dictates of my own wisdom and common-sense.

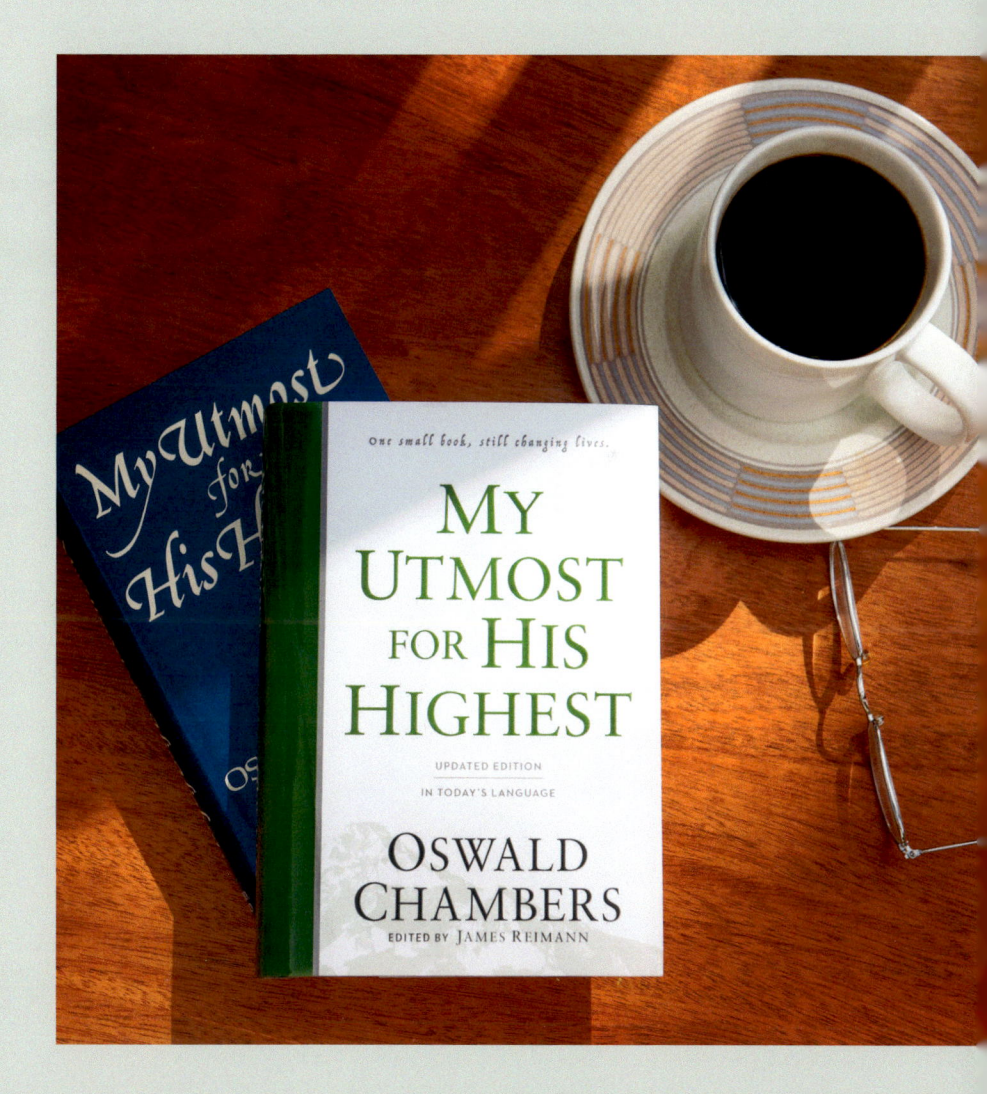

His Ongoing Ministry 155

TIMELINE OF OSWALD CHAMBERS'S LIFE AND WORK

1874–95	EARLY LIFE TO YOUNG ADULTHOOD
July 24, 1874	Born in Aberdeen, Scotland
Summer 1877	Family moves to Stoke-on-Trent, England
1881	Family moves to Perth, Scotland
September 1889	Family moves to London suburb of Peckham
December 2, 1890	Baptized and joins Rye Lane Baptist Chapel
April 29, 1893	Writes poem "Mental Depression"
Early 1895	Receives Art Master's Certificate and scholarship offer
February 27, 1895	Writes poem "Unemployed"
April 22, 1895	Writes of his perceived calling to the "aesthetic kingdom"
June 1895	Decides to enroll in two-year arts course at University of Edinburgh

1895–97	THE UNIVERSITY OF EDINBURGH
October 1895	Begins university studies
August 1, 1896	Letter to Chrissie Brain reveals financial difficulties
September 15, 1896	Writes poem "Hopeless"
October 1896	Friend's father says Oswald should be in the ministry
November 1896	Senses a call to the ministry; receives report from Dunoon College
February 16, 1897	Leaves for Dunoon

1897–1907	DUNOON COLLEGE
Late 1897	Becomes tutor at Dunoon
1897–1901	Years of "hell on earth," awaiting answer to plea for Holy Spirit
May 1899	Ordained to the ministry
May 4, 1898	Leads college when Duncan MacGregor is injured in fall
1901	Becomes involved with the League of Prayer
September 30, 1901	Writes poems "Fruitless Sorrow" and "Prayer Pleading"
November 1901	Experiences "entire sanctification"
Christmas 1905	Preaches in brother Arthur's church; meets Gertrude Hobbs
May 1906	Meets Juji Nakada; both speak at League of Prayer conference
Autumn 1906	Oswald and Nakada visit churches and League meetings throughout England and Scotland

1906–07	**TRAVEL TO UNITED STATES AND JAPAN**
November 6–15, 1906	Oswald and Nakada sail to the United States
December 21, 1906	Arrives in Cincinnati, Ohio
January 4, 1907	Begins teaching at God's Bible School
February 1907	Speaks in Providence, Rhode Island; visits Niagara Falls
April 1907	Visits Columbus, Ohio, with Quaker evangelist Charles Stalker
Late May 1907	In North Carolina for camp meetings
June 1, 1907	Begins first camp meeting in Cincinnati
July 10–27, 1907	Sails for Japan
Late August 1907	Leaves Japan to return to England

1907–10	**THE LEAGUE OF PRAYER**
November 1907–May 1908	On League business throughout the UK
May 28, 1908	Sails for America on the SS *Baltic*, along with Gertrude Hobbs
June 21, 1908	Begins camp meetings in Cincinnati
July 1908	Visits North Attleboro, Massachusetts and Old Orchard, Maine
August 1908	Back in England on League of Prayer business
October 18, 1908	Asks Mrs. Hobbs to correspond with Biddy; says "I love her"
October 23, 1908	Writes to Biddy, "I have nothing to offer you but my love"
October 28, 1908	Writes his parents about his love for Biddy
November 13, 1908	Oswald and Biddy engaged at St. Paul's Cathedral
November 1908	Ten-day mission in Belfast, Northern Ireland; meets Miss Ashe
December 1908–March 1909	On League business in Northern Ireland, Scotland, England
Late May 1909	Leaves for America aboard the *Lusitania*
June–July 1909	In Brooklyn, Cincinnati, and Old Orchard, Maine
Early August 1909	Returns to England
Late August 1909	In Aberdeen and Dundee, Scotland
Winter–Spring 1909	In London, Bristol, Plymouth, Dover, Gravesend, and Guisbrough
May 25, 1910	Oswald and Biddy married in London
Early June 1910	Newlyweds sail for America aboard the *Caronia*
June–September 1910	In Ohio, Massachusetts, Maryland, Maine, and the Catskills
September 21–29, 1910	Oswald and Biddy return to England aboard the *Adriatic*

1911–15	BIBLE TRAINING COLLEGE
Early December 1910	League of Prayer rents a building for the Bible Training College
January 12, 1911	The Bible Training College opens
January–June 1911	Teaching Biblical Psychology in three cities while leading B.T.C.
July 17–21, 1911	Oswald speaks at League of Prayer convention, Perth, Scotland
September 1911	Leads mission in Belfast; renews acquaintance with Miss Ashe
1912	*Biblical Psychology* published (US)
May 24, 1913	Birth of Kathleen Marian Chambers
September 28, 1913	Warns Biddy of allowing the baby to interfere with God's call
May 24, 1915	Writes to parents to say he is volunteering as front-line chaplain
July 14, 1915	B.T.C. closes at end of term
August 1915	The Chambers family and B.T.C. students vacation in Yorkshire
September 1915	Ministers to soldiers in Wensleydale training camps

1915–17	THE Y.M.C.A. IN EGYPT
October 9–26, 1915	Sails for Cairo, Egypt
October 27, 1915	First visit to Zeitoun camp; begins working almost immediately
November 17, 1915	Writes to tell Biddy to sail for Egypt
November 19, 1915	Receives permission to build his family home, the Bungalow
December 10–27, 1915	Biddy, Kathleen, and Mary Riley travel to join Oswald in Egypt
March 23–April 2, 1916	Conducts services in Ismailia, Moascar, Suez, and Wardan
Mid-May 1916	Assigned to Canal Zone when Zeitoun is emptied of troops
July 1, 1916	Biddy, Kathleen, and Mary Riley join Oswald at Ismailia
September 18, 1916	Chambers family leaves Ismailia for Zeitoun, with a ten-day vacation at Alexandria en route
January 14, 1917	Begins weekly service at Aotea Convalescent Home
January 30, 1917	Y.M.C.A. asks Oswald to stay at Zeitoun rather than return to England
Late July 1917	Oswald and Biddy begin six-day vacation in Damietta
October 17, 1917	Suffers an attack of appendicitis
October 29, 1917	Undergoes emergency appendectomy at Gizeh Red Cross Hospital
November 4, 1917	Experiences a blood clot in the lung
November 13, 1917	Begins hemorrhaging from the lung
November 15, 1917	Death, around 7 a.m.
November 16, 1917	Funeral in Cairo, Egypt; Biddy, Kathleen, and Eva Spink leave for two weeks in Luxor and Wasta
November 18, 1917	Memorial service at Zeitoun
November 30, 1917	Biddy and Kathleen return to Zeitoun

1917– HIS ONGOING MINISTRY

Early December 1917	Jimmy Hanson suggests printing Oswald Chambers leaflets for soldiers
December 1917	*Baffled to Fight Better* published
1918	*The Shadow of an Agony* published
July 3, 1919	Kathleen and Biddy return to England
1921	*Biblical Psychology* published (Britain)
1922	*The Psychology of Redemption* published
1924	Biddy and Kathleen move to Oxford; *Shade of His Hand* published
1927	*My Utmost for His Highest* published
1929	Biddy moves to London; *Our Brilliant Heritage* published
1933	*Oswald Chambers: His Life and Work* published
December 29, 1940	German firebombing destroys entire stock of 40,000 Oswald Chambers books
1942	Oswald Chambers Publications Association incorporated
January 15, 1966	Biddy Chambers dies
1968	*Oswald Chambers: An Unbribed Soul* by David Lambert published
1993	*Oswald Chambers: Abandoned to God* by David McCasland published
May 30, 1997	Kathleen Chambers dies
2000	*The Complete Works of Oswald Chambers* published
2008	*Searching for Mrs. Oswald Chambers* by Martha Christian published
2017	*Oswald Chambers: A Life in Pictures* by Paul Kent, *Mrs. Oswald Chambers: The Woman Behind the World's Bestselling Devotional* by Michelle Ule, and *My Utmost: A Devotional Memoir* by Macy Halford published

BIBLIOGRAPHY:
The Complete Works of Oswald Chambers

Approved unto God (1936), combined volume (1946) includes *Facing Reality*
> Investigates the need for spiritual fitness and true belief as Christians pursue service for God.

As He Walked (1930), see *Our Brilliant Heritage*

Baffled to Fight Better (1917)
> Study of the book of Job examines the problem of suffering. Now published under the title *Our Ultimate Refuge*.

Biblical Ethics (1947)
> Compilation of Oswald Chambers's teachings on ethics and Christian morality.

Biblical Psychology (US 1912; UK 1921)
> Marrying biblical studies and twentieth-century psychology, this book presents a biblical perspective on concepts such as the soul, spirit, and personality.

Bringing Sons unto Glory (1944)
> Studies of the life of Christ examining the meaning of His bodily incarnation for Christians today.

Called of God (1936), selections from *My Utmost for His Highest*
> Presents Oswald Chambers's views on the missionary call of the Christian.

Christian Disciplines, Vol. 1 (1965)
> Compilation of booklets exploring three Christian disciplines: divine guidance, suffering, and peril.

Christian Disciplines, Vol. 2 (1965)
> Compilation of booklets exploring three Christian disciplines: prayer, loneliness, and patience.

Conformed to His Image (1950)
> Collection of sermons and booklets on the Christian's pursuit of Christlikeness.

Disciples Indeed (1955)
> Described as a "handbook of sainthood," presents short and practical devotionals on topics including prayer, redemption, and testimony.

Facing Reality (1939), see *Approved unto God*

The Fighting Chance (1935), see *The Servant as His Lord*

Gems from Genesis (1989), combined volume of *Not Knowing Whither* and *Our Portrait in Genesis*

God's Workmanship (1953)
> One of the last books compiled by Biddy Chambers, this miscellaneous collection explores practical questions of Christian living.

The Graciousness of Uncertainty (1938), see ***The Love of God***

Grow Up into Him (1931), see ***Our Brilliant Heritage***

He Shall Glorify Me (1946)
> Lectures describe the person and work of the Holy Spirit, followed by themes including joy, forgiveness, and discipleship.

The Highest Good (1938), later editions include ***The Pilgrim's Songbook*** and ***Thy Great Redemption***
> Includes Oswald Chambers's teachings on Christian ethics, the doctrine of redemption, and the Psalms of Ascent.

If Thou Wilt Be Perfect (1939)
> Shares Chambers's insights as both a student and teacher of moral philosophy and Christian mysticism.

If Ye Shall Ask (1937)
> Lectures distill Chambers's wisdom on prayer, answering common questions about its purpose and practice. Now published under the title *If You Will Ask*.

Knocking at God's Door (1957), expanded edition of ***A Little Book of Prayers***
> Personal prayers from Chambers's journals, offering readers a prayer for each day of the year.

A Little Book of Prayers (1938), later expanded into ***Knocking at God's Door***

The Love of God (1938), combined volume (1965) includes ***The Ministry of the Unnoticed***, ***The Message of Invincible Consolation***, ***The Making of a Christian***, ***Now Is It Possible***, and ***The Graciousness of Uncertainty***
> Examines the heart of God's character and asks how His followers can live out love, faith, and holiness in both ordinary and difficult circumstances.

The Making of a Christian (1918, 1935), see ***The Love of God***

The Message of Invincible Consolation (1931), see ***The Love of God***

The Ministry of the Unnoticed (1936), see ***The Love of God***

The Moral Foundations of Life (1936)
> Study of ethical principles such as free will and grace, taking readers below the surface of Christian living.

My Utmost for His Highest (UK 1927, US 1935)
> Chambers's most enduring classic offers daily devotional readings to foster practical Christian living.

Notes on Ezekiel (1949, first time in book form in *The Complete Works of Oswald Chambers*, 2000)
    Lectures offer exposition on the first 34 chapters of Ezekiel.

Notes on Isaiah (1941, first time in book form in *The Complete Works of Oswald Chambers*, 2000)
    Lectures on the first 53 chapters of Isaiah investigate the character of God as revealed to His prophet.

Notes on Jeremiah (1936, first time in book form in *The Complete Works of Oswald Chambers*, 2000)
    Lectures on the first 29 chapters of Jeremiah explore God's relationship with His people.

Not Knowing Whither (1934)
    Lectures on the life of Abraham explore the challenges of faith and facing the unknown as Christians pursue friendship with God.

Now Is It Possible (1923, 1934), see *The Love of God*

Our Brilliant Heritage (1929), combined volume (1965) includes *Grow Up into Him* and *As He Walked*
    Delving into discipleship, moral philosophy, and the doctrine of sanctification, Chambers examines what it means to cultivate the habit of holiness.

Our Portrait in Genesis (1957)
    Exposition of the book of Genesis reflecting on the beginning of God's creation and His project of redemption for fallen humankind.

The Patience of the Saints (1939), see *The Servant as His Lord*

The Philosophy of Sin (1937)
    Studies of humanity's moral life examining sin and its remedy; both human need and God's redemptive provision to meet it.

The Pilgrim's Songbook (1940), see *The Highest Good*

The Place of Help (1935)
    Sermons address practical issues of Christian living such as fellowship, rest, and discipleship.

The Psychology of Redemption (1922)
    Draws parallels between the life of Christ and the Christian's life of faith, revealing how holy character is to be developed.

Run Today's Race (1968)
    Offers a daily "seed thought"—Chambers's term for pithy sayings designed to stimulate spiritual growth.

The Sacrament of Saints (1934), see *The Servant as His Lord*

The Saints in the Disaster of Worldliness (1939), see *The Servant as His Lord*

The Servant as His Lord (1959), combined volume includes ***The Fighting Chance***, ***The Soul of a Christian***, ***The Saints in the Disaster of Worldliness***, and ***The Sacrament of Saints***
> Compilation of booklets presenting different aspects of the Christian's pursuit of Christlikeness, including perseverance, sacrifice, and intimacy with God.

Shade of His Hand (1924)
> Based on the book of Ecclesiastes, Chambers's final lectures affirm that life is not worth living apart from God's redeeming love.

The Shadow of an Agony (1918)
> Collection of talks investigating the tragedies of life and the mystery of suffering.

So Send I You (1930)
> Explores the call and preparation of the missionary, offering insights on the use of spiritual discernment to serve those around us.

The Soul of a Christian (1936), see ***The Servant as His Lord***

Studies in the Sermon on the Mount (1915), expanded edition (1929)
> Study of Matthew 5–7 invites readers to hear the beatitudes not simply as the words of Jesus the teacher but as the call of Jesus the savior.

Thy Great Redemption (1937), see ***The Highest Good***

Workmen of God (1937)
> Examines how Christians can use spiritual discernment to diagnose and deal with the spiritual conditions of others.

SOURCES

Archives

Oswald Chambers Papers, 1886–1983, Wheaton College Archives and Special Collections.

Books

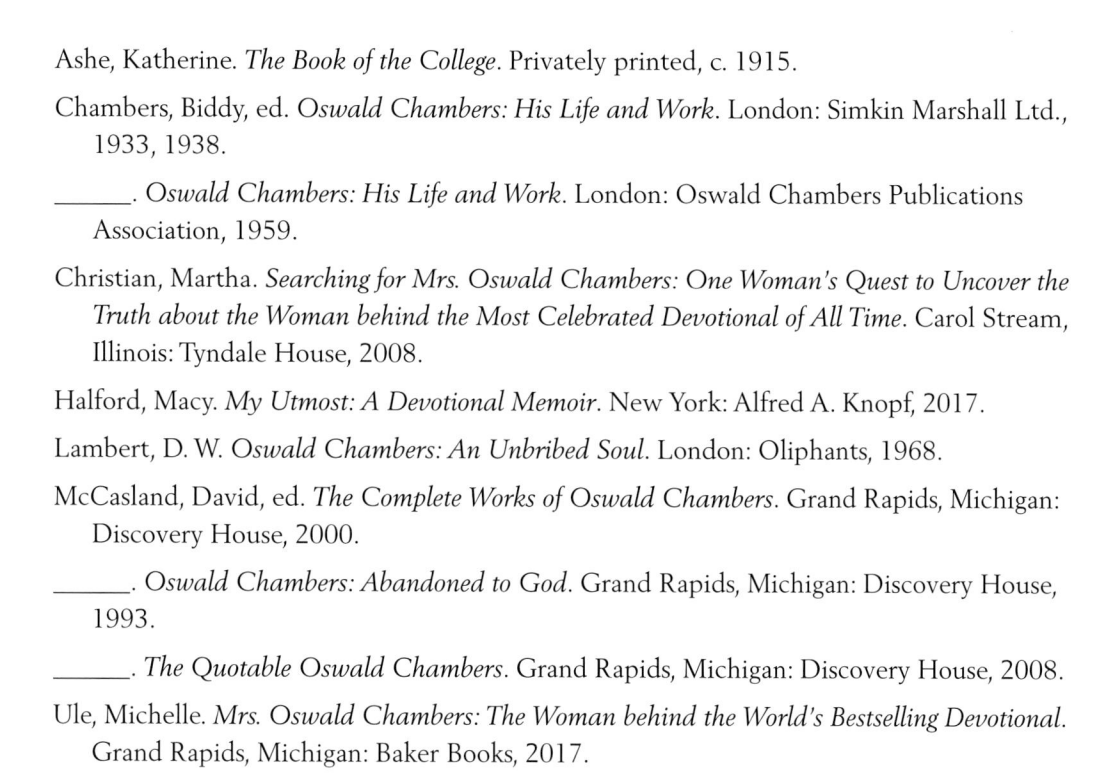

Ashe, Katherine. *The Book of the College*. Privately printed, c. 1915.

Chambers, Biddy, ed. *Oswald Chambers: His Life and Work*. London: Simkin Marshall Ltd., 1933, 1938.

_____. *Oswald Chambers: His Life and Work*. London: Oswald Chambers Publications Association, 1959.

Christian, Martha. *Searching for Mrs. Oswald Chambers: One Woman's Quest to Uncover the Truth about the Woman behind the Most Celebrated Devotional of All Time*. Carol Stream, Illinois: Tyndale House, 2008.

Halford, Macy. *My Utmost: A Devotional Memoir*. New York: Alfred A. Knopf, 2017.

Lambert, D. W. *Oswald Chambers: An Unbribed Soul*. London: Oliphants, 1968.

McCasland, David, ed. *The Complete Works of Oswald Chambers*. Grand Rapids, Michigan: Discovery House, 2000.

_____. *Oswald Chambers: Abandoned to God*. Grand Rapids, Michigan: Discovery House, 1993.

_____. *The Quotable Oswald Chambers*. Grand Rapids, Michigan: Discovery House, 2008.

Ule, Michelle. *Mrs. Oswald Chambers: The Woman behind the World's Bestselling Devotional*. Grand Rapids, Michigan: Baker Books, 2017.

DVDs

Day of Discovery. *My Utmost for His Highest: The Legacy of Oswald and Biddy Chambers*. Grand Rapids, Michigan: Our Daily Bread Ministries, 2011.

PHOTOGRAPHY CREDITS

Unless otherwise noted, all photographs are used by permission of the Wheaton College Archives and Special Collections.

Other photograph contributors:

Cover inset photographs (typewriter and tools, pocket watch, Bible) and pages 8 (typewriter), 31 (Bible), 146, 149 (book), 150, 151, 153 (book): Terry Bidgood © Our Daily Bread Ministries

Cover image, inset left, and pages 52–53: Shutterstock/Phill Beale

Pages 10: Shutterstock/s_karau

Pages 12 (Oswald and Gertrude), 51: Mrs. Barbara (Chambers) Penn

Page 15: Shutterstock/Stephen McClusky

Page 23: commons.wikimedia.org/wiki/File:MetropolitanTabernacleSouth.jpg by Secretlondon, licensed under Creative Commons 1.0

Page 30: Shutterstock/Foppe Smit

Page 33: ThinkstockPhotos/Shaiith

Page 38: Shutterstock/James Greenshields

Pages 41, 67 (Chambers portrait): Oswald Chambers Publications Association, Limited

Pages 46–47: Shutterstock/TreasureGalore

Page 58: Shutterstock/Dave Allen Photography

Pages 61, 62, 68, 69: God's Bible School and College

Page 63: Shutterstock/Sean Pavone

Page 64: Shutterstock/Jim Pruitt

Page 67 (R.M.S. *Baltic*): Heritage-Ships

Pages 70–71: Shutterstock/Vlad Siaber

Page 73: Shutterstock/Anna Bogush

Page 84: Shutterstock/Kiev.Victor

Page 87: Shutterstock/Avella

Page 88: Shutterstock/Vividrange

Page 93 (passenger list): British National Archives

Pages 94–95: Shutterstock/Alexey Smolyanyy

Page 96: iStockphoto/_ultraforma_

Page 112: ThinkstockPhotos/CaronB

Page 120: iStockphoto/AskinTulayOver

Pages 125, 142: Cadbury Research Library, University of Birmingham, used by permission of YMCA England & Wales

Pages 136–137: Shutterstock/Pikoso.kz

Pages 144–145: *Day of Discovery* © Our Daily Bread Ministries

Back jacket flap: St. Paul Cathedral, Shutterstock/Kiev.Victor